DYING THOUGHTS

DYING THOUGHTS

Richard Baxter

'For I am in a strait betwixt two, having a desire to depart, and to be with Christ; which is far better' (*Phil.* 1:23).

THE BANNER OF TRUTH TRUST

THE BANNER OF TRUTH TRUST
3 Murrayfield Road, Edinburgh EH12 6EL, UK
P.O. Box 621, Carlisle, PA 17013, USA

*

First published 1683
This edition based on the abridgement
by Benjamin Fawcett 1761

© Banner of Truth Trust 2004
Reprinted 2009 (twice)
Reprinted 2016

ISBN: 978 0 85151 886 2

*

Typeset in 10.5/14 pt Sabon Oldstyle Figures at
the Banner of Truth Trust, Edinburgh

Printed in the USA by
Versa Press, Inc.,
East Peoria, IL

Contents

INTRODUCTION

Richard Baxter – A Corrective for Reformed Preachers [1]

Edward Donnelly

Baxter is no more of a perfect exemplar than any other son of Adam. His theology was flawed. His desire to promote church unity sometimes betrayed him into seeking common cause with those who were far removed from biblical faith. Although an able controversialist, he confesses: 'I am too much inclined to such words in controversial writings which are too keen, and apt to provoke the person whom I write against.' In looking for help from the Puritan giants, are there not other and safer preaching models?

The answer lies in his particular value for our present needs. In the providence of God a renewed interest in Reformed truth has led to an increased number of men

[1] First published in the Banner of Truth magazine, No. 166–7 (July-August 1977), pp. 6–12.

raised up to preach the doctrines of grace. But any new development may run to extremes, and there is always the danger that a preacher, in the first flush of enthusiasm for what he has discovered, may, in his very efforts to be thoroughly Reformed, become a caricature of that which he admires. It is precisely here that Baxter can help us, for, where he is strong, too many today are weak. Three characteristics of his preaching in particular speak to our current situation.

1. *Baxter's preaching was devoted to a simple explanation of basic truths.*

He believed that a preacher should reason with his hearers. 'We should be furnished with all kind of evidence so that we may come as with a torrent upon their understandings, and with our reasonings and expostulations to pour shame upon their vain objections, and bear down all before us, that they may be forced to yield to the power of truth.' Though well aware of the darkness of the unregenerate mind, he was always concerned to explain what he was saying and to clear up possible misunderstandings. His sermons had a logical structure – first the 'opening' of the text, then the removal of difficulties, followed by the 'uses' and the appeal. Even in the middle of the most impassioned pleading he constantly enlisted the aid of reason. After beseeching with great tenderness and power at the close of *Making Light of Christ and Salvation*, he ends by enumerating nine false grounds of assurance, followed by eight tests by which his hearers may prove their own sincerity. A rhetorician would cringe at such squandering of 'emotional impact', but Baxter was content to let the truth make its own impact, and he was preaching firstly to teach his hearers and only then to move them.

The truths preached were the fundamentals. 'Throughout the whole course of our ministry, we must insist chiefly upon the greatest, most certain and most necessary truths, and be more seldom and sparing upon the rest . . . Many other things are desirable to be known, but some must be known, or else our people are undone for ever.' This, however, was not a blinkered concentration on a few well-trodden passages. Baxter covered all of Scripture. He dealt deeply and argued closely. He set forth these fundamentals in all the fulness of their interrelationship and application. But he believed that preaching should meet people's needs, that it failed if their greatest needs were not met, and that the 'matters of necessity' should be at the forefront.

The great fundamentals were taught in simple language, for 'there is no better way to make a good cause prevail than to make it plain'. Since the purpose of the preacher was to teach, he must speak so as to be understood. In those days of sermon-tasters he was criticized for the plainness of his speech and had to combat the pride of his heart as it urged him to a more ornate style:

God commandeth us to be as plain as we can, that we may inform the ignorant . . . but pride stands by and contradicteth all, and produceth its toys and trifles . . . It persuadeth us to paint the window that it may dim the light.

Such painstaking logic and principled simplicity are a challenge to modern preachers. We aim at giving reasoned expositions of truth to our people, but do we, in preparation, seek to answer any possible difficulties, do we marshal arguments to convince their minds – or have we been made lazy by their uncritical approval? Are we so afraid of being labelled 'fundamentalists' that we spend most of our time in the lesser-known corners of Scripture? It is possible for a man to win a reputation as the manager of a delicatessen for Reformed gourmets, producing theological rarities which are unobtainable elsewhere – while many of his hungry flock look up and are not fed. It is a tragic mistake so to concentrate on 'what is desirable to be known' that we neglect 'what must be known'. Do our people really understand the central truths concerning the being of God, Christ's person and work, sin, regeneration, repentance and faith? Until the foundations of their faith are firmly established, we do well to lay less emphasis upon superstructure.

Do we preach in simple language? No doubt we try to avoid over-academic expressions, and it is quite true that many of the great terms of Scripture need to be expounded and then incorporated into the thinking and speech of our hearers. But do we make the enormous conscious effort necessary to avoid the thought-benumbing cliché, to present the truth in fresh, contemporary clothing? Baxter calls us to a preaching ministry in which the fundamentals of the faith are explained logically and clearly.

2. *Baxter's preaching was characterized by a passionate evangelistic appeal.*

The great reality which moulded his ministry was the fact that we must all appear before the judgment seat of Christ. Extreme bodily weakness increased his awareness that there was but a step between him and death, whom he called his 'neighbour'. Every duty was to be carried out, every sermon preached, in the light of the great day. 'I daily know and think of that approaching hour', he says. His congregation is described as 'a company of ignorant, carnal, miserable sinners . . . who must be changed or damned. Methinks I even see them entering upon their final woe! Methinks I hear them crying out for help, for speediest help!'

This awareness of eternity made Baxter an emotional preacher. 'If you want to know the art of pleading' said Spurgeon, 'read Baxter.' Yet his emotion was not undisciplined, but fuelled by his comprehension of truth, for he had no time for 'an affected fervency'. 'Light first, then heat', was his motto – first the exposition of truth, then the words of piercing appeal springing from that truth. At the close of *A Call to the Unconverted to Turn and Live* he appeals to his hearers with such tender earnestness that we can almost see the tears upon his cheeks. 'My heart is troubled to think how I shall leave you, lest . . .

I should leave you as I found you, till you awake in hell
. . . I am as hearty a beggar with you this day, for the
saving of your souls, as I would be for my own supply,
if I were forced to come a begging to your doors. And
therefore if you would hear me then, hear me now. If you
would pity me then, be entreated now to pity yourselves
. . . O sirs, believe it, death and judgment, heaven and
hell, are other matters when you come near them, than
they seem to carnal eyes afar off. Then you will hear such
a message as I bring you with more awakened, regardful
hearts.'

The focus of his preaching was an urgent invitation to
receive Christ. Baxter preached for a verdict. He sought to
'drive sinners to a stand and make them see . . . that they
must unavoidably be either converted or condemned.' His
words at the close of *Making Light of Christ and Salvation* are pointed and powerful:

When God hath shaken those careless souls out of their
bodies, and you must answer for all your sins in your
own name; Oh, then what would you give for a Saviour!
. . .When you see the world hath left you, and your companions in sin have deceived themselves and you, and
all your merry days are gone; then what would you give
for that Christ and salvation that now you account not
worth your labour! . . . You that cannot make light of a
little sickness, or of want, or of natural death, no, not of
a toothache, but groan as if you were undone; how will
you then make light of the fury of the Lord, which will

burn against the contemners of His grace? I come now to know your resolution for the time to come. What say you? Do you mean to set as light by Christ and salvation as hitherto you have done and to be the same men after all this? I hope not.

The sharp edge was always present – a choice had to be made, a verdict given, an offer of mercy accepted or rejected.

Yet this is far removed from shallow decisionism. Some preachers seem afraid of letting their hearers 'get away', determined as they are to manipulate them to a 'decision for Christ' before second thoughts can quench newly-awakened enthusiasm. Not only was Baxter not afraid of second thoughts, he was counting on them, hoping that his hearers would reflect deeply upon what had been preached. So we find him planting time-bombs in the minds of his people, applications which would continue to speak after his voice had fallen silent:

I cannot now follow you to your several habitations to apply this word to your particular necessities, but Oh, that I might make every man's conscience a preacher to himself, that it might do it, which is ever with you! That the next time you go prayerless to bed, or about your business, conscience might cry out, Dost thou set no more by Christ and thy salvation? . . . That the next time you are ready to rush upon known sin . . . conscience might cry out, Is Christ and salvation no more worth, than to cast them away, or venture them for thy lusts? . . . That when you are next spending the Lord's day in idleness or vain sports, conscience might tell you what you are doing.

He takes each facet of life and enlists it as a preacher, so that the sinner may be hemmed in by an environment in which every part declares the claims of God.

Whether fairly or not, Reformed preachers have a reputation for being restrained and impersonal in their delivery. It may be a reaction against the excesses of a dumbed-down, touchy-feely age, against zeal without knowledge, heat without light, sound without sense. But has it become an overreaction? Can we speak about the misery of human depravity and the wonder of sovereign grace, without being deeply moved by such tremendous realities? Has the development of our heads so shrivelled our hearts as to render us suspicious of genuine emotion? Or is the problem doctrinal? Do we hesitate to press the gospel upon people for fear of being thought Arminian? The 'five points' can be treated as a theological minefield through which the preacher tiptoes, so afraid of blowing himself up on the horns of a careless expression that he ceases to long for the conversion of his hearers. The life and impact of a sermon bleed away in the death of a thousand qualifications. But our preaching is a travesty if it lacks an earnest pleading with men to receive an all-sufficient Christ, freely offered to all who will come. The truths of Calvinism are not barriers which must be surmounted before the gospel can be preached, but a platform from which to preach more powerfully. It is precisely because grace is sovereign and free that we can urge it passionately – because the redemption purchased by Christ is complete and certain that we can commend it so glowingly – because God has chosen some out of His mere good pleasure that we can preach confidently. If we are to stand in the line of biblical, Reformed preachers, we will take note of this element in Baxter's preaching.

3. *Baxter's preaching was shaped and enforced by systematic pastoral counselling.*

He made no division between preaching and pastoral work, for he understood what Paul meant when he reminded the Ephesians that he had taught them 'publicly and from house to house'. The task is one – the same truth communicated to the same people for the same end – the glory of God through their salvation or condemnation. And this perhaps is where Baxter may prove most serviceable to the ministers of today – in the forging of a strong link between pulpit and pastorate.

Baxter expected conversions to result from his preaching. He advised his brother ministers: 'If you long not to see the conversion and edification of your hearers, and do not preach and study in hope, you are not likely to see much success.' While depending wholly upon the Lord for success, he attacked with all his might the callous sleight-of-hand by which God's sovereignty in granting or withholding blessing can be used as a cloak for indifference. The preacher must long for the conversion of his hearers and be filled with grief if they do not respond:

I know that a faithful minister may have comfort when he lacks success . . . but then, he that longeth not for the success of his labours can have none of this comfort, because he was not a faithful labourer . . . What if God will accept a physician though the patient die? He must, notwithstanding that, work in compassion, and long for a better issue and be sorry if he miss it.

This longing for results drove him to the homes of his people and to the work of personal catechizing. He wanted to discover how much of the preaching they had understood, what effect it had had upon them, whether or not they had embraced the gospel offer of mercy. Did the seed which he had sown need further cultivation ? Were there weeds to be removed from the soil?

These questions could be answered only in personal conversation. At first, he shrank from the work: 'Many of us have a foolish bashfulness, which makes us backward to begin with them, and to speak plainly to them' – but, as he gained experience, this pastoral counselling became 'the most comfortable work, except public preaching, that ever I yet did set my hand to.' It must be stressed that it was his earnestness as a preacher which made him such a diligent pastor. His home visitation was a means of expanding and further applying what had been said in the pulpit. He found indeed that people would not take his preaching seriously unless it was enforced by close personal dealing. In a classic passage from the *Reformed Pastor* he says:

They will give you leave to preach against their sins, and
to talk as much as you will for godliness in the pulpit, if
you will but let them alone afterwards, and be friendly
and merry with them when you have done . . . For they
take the pulpit to be a stage; a place where preachers
must show themselves and play their parts; where you
have liberty for an hour to say what you list; and what
you say they regard not, if you show them not, by saying
it personally to their faces, that you were in good earnest
and did indeed mean them.

His pastoral work not only enforced his past preaching
but helped him to preach more pointedly and relevantly
in the future. 'It will furnish you with useful matter for
your sermons, to talk an hour with an ignorant or obstinate sinner, as much as an hour's study will do, for
you will learn what you have need to insist on and what
objections of theirs to repel.' He got to know his people
– their personalities, problems, temptations, way of life.
He sat where they sat and was thus enabled to preach
sermons which were tailored to their peculiar needs.

Several eminent Reformed preachers have recently
provided specious justifications for downplaying the
importance of day-to-day contact with our people. But
in order to be a true preacher a man must be a true
pastor. It is all too possible – and comfortable – to mis-
use the centrality of preaching as an excuse for pastoral
cowardice or neglect. Does the fact of having preached
publicly against our people's sins absolve us from the

responsibility of speaking to them in their homes about those same sins? We are called to be diligent students, to labour in the Word, to be much in the secret place. But the study may become a convenient refuge from reality and we may all too easily salve our consciences over an unpaid visit by reading yet another book. Many of us have discovered, to our shame, that the courage with which we have preached can evaporate during the walk to the door of the meeting-house. Having thundered boldly from the pulpit, we have found ourselves trying to conciliate with an especially warm smile or handshake those very individuals whose consciences we were seeking to wound, 'to be friendly and merry with them', to prefer that God should be angry with them than that they should be angry with us.

In attempting to stress the importance of preaching, it is possible to over-react by minimizing personal work. Personal counselling can be no substitute for the preached Word, but, as a means of enforcing and applying that Word to the individual conscience, it fulfils a unique function. It will also serve to make us better preachers – not worse. As we go from house to house, the mists of bookishness will be blown away and we will return to prepare sermons which are rooted in the life and language of the people.

This then is Richard Baxter of Kidderminster. A preacher who laboured to make plain the truth of God, who spoke from a burning heart as he pleaded with his people to close with Christ. A pastor who knew his sheep by name, who spoke to them personally about the great concerns of their souls. He is not merely an historical curiosity, a fossil to be marvelled at, but a stimulus, a rebuke, an encouragement. In his *Dying Thoughts,* he lays bare the preacher's heart:

> My Lord, I have nothing to do in this world, but to seek and serve thee; I have nothing to do with a heart and its affections but to breathe after thee; I have nothing to do with my tongue and pen, but to speak to thee, and for thee, and to publish thy glory and thy will.

I

WHAT THERE IS DESIRABLE IN THE PRESENT LIFE

'Man that is born of a woman, is of few days, and full of trouble: he cometh forth like a flower, and is cut down: he fleeth also as a shadow, and continueth not.' 'And dost thou open thine eyes upon such an one, and bringest me into judgment with thee?' As a watch, when it is wound up, or a candle newly lighted; so man, newly conceived or born, begins a motion which incessantly hastes to its appointed period. And as an action, or the time of it, is nothing when it is past; so vain a thing would man be, and so vain is life, were it not for the hopes of a more durable life with which this is connected. But those hopes, and the means for supporting them, do not only distinguish a believer from an infidel, but a man from a beast. When Solomon describes the difference, only in respect to time and the things of time, he well observes that one event happening to both, shows that both are vanity. And Paul says of Christians, 'If in this life only we have hope, we are of all men most miserable.' Though even in this life, as related to a better, and as we ourselves are exercised about things of a higher nature than the concerns of a temporal life, we are far happier than the men of the world.

2. I am intending to speak to none but myself, and therefore (supposing the meaning of the text[1] to be duly ascertained) shall only observe what is useful to my own heart and practice. In this chapter, I will consider, *What there is desirable in the present life*; then show, Chapter 2, *The necessity and reasonableness of believing that pious separate spirits are with Christ*; next explain, Chapter 3, *What it is to depart, and to be with Christ*; and, Chapter 4, *Why it is far better to be with him.* I will conclude, Chapter 5, with expressing my concern *that I myself may be willing to depart, and to be with Christ.*

3. It was a happy state into which grace had brought the apostle, who saw so much of what was not only tolerable, but greatly desirable, both in living and dying. 'For him to live was Christ'; that is, to do the work, and serve the interest of Christ: for him 'to die was gain'; that is, would be his own interest and reward. His strait was not, whether it would be good to live, or good to depart, because both were good; but he doubted which of the two were more desirable. Nor was it his meaning,

---

[1] 'For I am in a strait betwixt two, having a desire to depart, and to be with Christ; which is far better' (*Phil.* 1:23).

to bring his own interest and Christ's into competition with each other. By Christ, or the interest of Christ, he means his serving the churches of Christ upon earth. But he knew that Christ had an interest also in his saints above; and could raise up more to serve him here. Yet, because he was to judge by what appeared, and saw that such were much wanted upon earth, this turned the scales in his choice; and therefore, in order to serve Christ in the edification of his churches, he was more inclined, by denying himself, to have his reward delayed; at this same time well knowing that the delay of his reward would tend to its increase. Here let me observe that, *even in this world short of death, there is some good so much to be regarded, as may justly prevail with believers to prefer it before the present hasting of their reward.*

I rather note this, that no temptation may carry me into the extreme of taking nothing but heaven to be worth minding; and so even sinfully cast off the world, on pretence of mortification and a heavenly life. Not that any thing on earth is better than heaven, or in itself to be preferred before heaven. The end, as such, is better than the means, and perfection better than imperfection. But the present use of the means may be sometimes preferred before the present possession of the end. And the use of the means for a higher end, may be preferred before the present possession of a lower end. Every thing has its season. Planting, sowing, and building, are not so good as reaping, fruit-gathering, and dwelling; but in their season, they must be first done.

4. But let me inquire, *What is there so desirable in this present life?* The answer is obvious: for,

i. While this present life continues, the will of God is fulfilled, who will have us upon earth for a season; and that is best which God wills.

ii. The life to come depends upon this present life. As the life of adult age depends upon infancy, or the reward upon the work; or the prize of racers or soldiers upon their running or fighting; or the merchant's gain upon his voyage. Heaven is won or lost on earth; the possession is there, but the preparation is here. Christ will judge all men in another state, as their works have been in this. First, Well done, good and faithful servant; then, Enter thou into the joy of thy Lord. 'I have fought a good fight, I have finished my course,' must go before the crown of righteousness 'which the Lord, the righteous Judge, shall give.'

All that we ever do for salvation, must be done here. It was on earth that Christ himself wrought the work of our redemption, fulfilled all righteousness, became our ransom, and paid the price of our salvation; and here also must we do our part. The bestowing of the reward is God's work, who, we are sure, will never fail. Here is no room for the least suspicion of his failing in any thing he undertakes; but the danger and fear is of our own miscarrying, lest we be not found capable of receiving what God will certainly give to all that are fit to receive it. To distrust God, is heinous sin and folly; but to distrust ourselves is highly reasonable. So that if we will make sure of heaven, it must be by 'giving all diligence to make our calling and election sure' upon earth. If we fear hell, we must fear our being prepared for it. And it is great and difficult work we have to do upon earth; as, for instance, to be cured of all damning sin; to be born again; to be pardoned and justified by faith; to be united to Christ, made wise to salvation, renewed by his Spirit, and conformed to his likeness; to overcome all the temptations of the world, the flesh, and the devil; to perform all the duties toward God and man that must be rewarded; 'with the heart to believe in Christ unto righteousness, and with the mouth to make confession unto salvation'; also to 'suffer with Christ, that we may reign with him; and to be faithful to death, that we may receive the crown of life'. Thus on earth must we 'so run, that we may obtain'.

iii. We are members of the world and of the church, and must labour to do good to many; and therefore we have greater work to do on earth than merely securing our own salvation. We are entrusted with our Master's talents for his service, to do our best in our places, to propagate his truth and grace, to edify his church, honour his cause, and promote the salvation of as many souls as we can. All this is to be done on earth, if we would secure the end of all in heaven.

5. It is then an error, though but few are guilty of it, to think that all religion lies in minding only the life to come, and in disregarding all things in this present life. All true Christians must seriously mind both the end and the means of attaining it. If they believingly mind not the end,

they will never be faithful in the use of the means; if they be not diligent in using the means, they will never obtain the end. None can use earth well, that prefer not heaven; and none but infants can come to heaven, that are not prepared for it by well using earth. Heaven must have our highest esteem, and our habitual love, desire, and joy; but earth must have more of our daily thoughts for present practice. A man that travels to the most desirable home, has an habitual desire to it all the way; but his present business is his journey, and therefore his horse, inns, and company, his roads, and his fatigues, may employ more of his thoughts, and talk, and action, than his home.

6. I have often wondered to find David, in the Psalms, and other saints, before the coming of Christ, express so great a sense of the things of this present life, and say so little of another; making so much account of prosperity, dominion, and victories, on the one hand, and of persecution, and the success of enemies, on the other hand. But I consider, that it was not for mere personal and carnal interest, but for the church of God, and for his honour, Word, and worship; for they knew, if things go well with us on earth, they will be sure to go well in heaven; if the militant church prosper in holiness, there is no doubt but it will triumph in glory. Satan does much of his damning work by men, as his instruments; so that if we escape their temptations, we escape much of our danger. When idolaters prospered, Israel was tempted to idolatry. The Greek church is now almost swallowed up by Turkish

prosperity and dominion. Most follow the powerful and prosperous side. And therefore, for the glory of God, and for our own everlasting salvation, we must, while upon earth, greatly regard our own, and much more the church's welfare. Indeed, if earth be desired only for earth, and prosperity be loved only to gratify the flesh, it is the certain mark of damning carnality, and an earthly mind. But to desire peace and prosperity, and to have power in the hands of wise and faithful men, for the sake of souls, the increase of the church, and the honour of God, that 'his name may be hallowed, his kingdom come, and his will be done on earth, as it is in heaven' – this must be the chief of our prayers.

7. And now, O my soul! Be not unthankful for the mercies of this present life. This body is so nearly united to thee, that it must needs be a greater help or hindrance. Had it been more afflicted, it might have been a discouraging clog; like a tired horse in a journey, or an ill tool to a workman, or an untuned instrument in music. A sick or a bad servant in a house is a great trouble, and much more a bad wife: but thy body is nearer to thee than either of those could be, and will be more of thy concern. Yet if it had been more strong and healthful, sense and appetite would have been strong; and the stronger thy lusts, the greater would have been thy danger, and much more difficult thy victory and salvation. Even weak senses and temptations have too often prevailed. How knowest thou then what stronger might have done? When I see a thirsty

man in a fever, a dropsy; and especially when I see strong and healthful youths, bred up in fullness and among temptations, how they are mad in sin, violently carried to it, bearing down the rebukes of God and conscience, parents and friends, and all regard to their own salvation; this tells me how great a mercy I had, even in a body not liable to their case. Also, many a bodily deliverance has been of great use to my soul, renewing my time and opportunity, and strength for service, and bringing frequent and fresh reports of the love of God. If bodily mercies were not of great use to the soul, Christ would not so much have showed his saving love, as he did, by healing all manner of diseases. Nor would God promise us a resurrection of the body, if a suitable body did not promote the welfare of the soul.

8. I am obliged to great thankfulness to God, for the mercies of this life which he hath showed to my friends. That which promotes their joy, should increase mine. I ought 'to rejoice with them that rejoice'. Nature and grace teach us to be glad, when our friends are well and prosper; though all this must be in order to better things than bodily welfare.

9. Nor must I undervalue such mercies of this life as belong to the land of my nativity. The want of them are part of God's threatened curse; and 'godliness has a promise of the life that now is, and of that which is to come, and so is profitable unto all things'. When God sends on a land the plagues of pestilence, war, persecution, and famine,

especially a famine of the Word of God, it is a great sin to be insensible of them. If any shall say, 'While heaven is sure, we have no cause to accuse God, or to cast away comfort, hope, or duty,' they say well. But if they say, 'Because heaven is all, we must make light of all that befalls us on earth,' they say amiss. Good princes, magistrates, and public-spirited men, who promote the safety, peace, and true prosperity of the commonwealth, do thereby very much befriend religion, and men's salvation, and are greatly to be loved and honoured by all. If the civil state miscarry, or fall into ruin and calamity, the church will fare the worse for it, as the soul does by the ruins of the body. Religion consumes away, and falls into contempt, or withers into ceremony and formality, wheresoever tyranny brings slavery, beggary, or long persecution, upon the subjects. Let me, therefore be thankful for all the protection of magistracy, the plenty of preachers, the preservation from enemies, the restraint of persecution, the concord of Christians, and increase of godliness, in this land, and especially that the gospel is continued in it.

10. Be particularly thankful, O my soul! That God hath made any use of thee for the service of his church on earth. My God, my soul for this doth magnify thee, and my spirit rejoiceth in the review of thy great undeserved mercy. O what am I, whom thou tookest up from the dunghill, or low obscurity, that I should live myself in the constant relish of thy sweet and sacred truth, and with such encouraging success communicate it to others!

That I may say, now my public work seems ended, that these forty-three or forty-four years I have no reason to think that ever I laboured in vain! O with what gratitude must I look upon all places where I lived and laboured; but, above all, that place which had my strength![1] I bless thee for the great number of them gone to heaven, and for the continuance of piety, humility, concord, and peace, among them. Also for all that by my writings have received any saving light and grace. O my God, let not my own heart be barren, while I labour in thy husbandry to bring others unto holy fruit! Let me not be a stranger to the life and power of that saving truth, which I have done so much to communicate to others! O let not my own words and writings condemn me, as void of that divine and heavenly nature and life, which I have said so much of to the world!

11. Stir up then, O my soul, thy sincere desires, and all thy faculties, to do the remnant of the work of Christ appointed thee on earth, and then joyfully wait for the heavenly perfection in God's own time. Thou canst truly say, 'To me to live is Christ.' It is his work for which thou livest. Thou hast no other business in the world. But thou doest this work with a mixture of many oversights and imperfections, and too much troublest thy thoughts with distrust about God's part, who never fails. If thy work be done, be thankful for what is past, and that thou art come so near the port of rest. If God will add any more to thy days, serve him with double alacrity. The prize is al-

[1] Kidderminster

most within sight. Time is swift and short. Thou hast told others, that 'there is no working in the grave,' and that it must be now or never. Dream not, because Christ's righteousness was perfect, that God will save the wicked, or equally reward the slothful and the diligent. As sin is its own punishment, holiness is much of its own reward. Whatever God appointeth thee to do, see that thou do it sincerely, and with all thy might. If sin dispose men to be angry because it is detected, disgraced, and resisted; so that God be pleased, their wrath should be patiently borne, who will shortly be far more angry with themselves. I shall not be hurt, when I am with Christ, by the calumnies of men on earth; but the saving benefit will, by converted sinners, be enjoyed everlastingly. Words and actions are transient things, and being once past, are nothing; but the effect of them on an immortal soul may be endless. All the sermons that I have preached are nothing now; but the grace of God on sanctified souls is the beginning of eternal life.

It is an unspeakable mercy to be thus employed sincerely and with success; and therefore I had reason all this while to be in Paul's strait, and make no haste in my 'desires to depart'. The crown will come in its due time; and eternity is long enough to enjoy it, how long soever it be delayed. But if I will do that, which must obtain it for myself and others, it must be quickly done, before my declining sun be set. O that I had no worse causes of my unwillingness yet to die, than my desire to do the work of life for my own and other men's salvation, and to 'finish my course with joy, and the ministry I have received of the Lord'!

12. As it is on earth I must do good to others, so it must be in a manner suited to their earthly state. Souls are here closely united to bodies, by which they must receive much good or hurt. Do good to men's bodies, if thou wouldest do good to their souls. Say not, Things corporeal are worthless trifles, for which the receivers will be never the better. They are things that nature is easily sensible of, and sense is the passage to the mind and will. Dost thou not find what a help it is to thyself, to have at any time any ease and alacrity of body; and what a burden and hindrance pains and cares are? Labour then to free others from such burdens and temptations, and be not regardless of them. If thou must 'rejoice with them that rejoice, and weep with them that weep', promote then thy own joy by helping theirs; and avoid thy own sorrows, in preventing or curing theirs. But, alas! What power has selfishness in most? How easily do we bear our brethren's pains and reproaches, wants and afflictions, in comparison of our own! How few thoughts, and how little cost and labour, do we use for their supply, in comparison of what we do for ourselves! Nature indeed teaches us to be sensible of our own case; but grace tells us, that we should not make so great a difference as we do, but should love our neighbour as ourselves.

13. And now, O my soul, consider how mercifully God hath dealt with thee, that thy strait should be between two conditions so desirable. I shall either die speedily, or stay yet longer upon earth; whichever it be, it will be a merciful and comfortable state. That it is 'desirable to

depart, and be with Christ,' I must not doubt, and shall hereafter more copiously consider. And if my abode on earth yet longer be so great a mercy, as to be put into the balance against my present possession of heaven, surely it must be a state which obliges me to great thankfulness to God, and comfortable acknowledgement: nor should my pain, or sickness, or sufferings from men, make this life on earth unacceptable while God will continue me in it. Paul had his thorn in the flesh, the messenger of Satan to buffet him, and suffered more from men, though less in his health, than I have done; and yet he 'gloried in his infirmities, and rejoiced in his tribulations,' and was 'in a strait betwixt' living and dying; yea, rather chose to live yet longer.

Alas! The strait of most men is between the desire of life for fleshly interest, and the fear of death as ending their felicity; between a tiring world and body, which makes them weary of living, and the dreadful prospect of future danger, which makes them afraid of dying. If they live, it is in misery; if they must die, they fear greater misery: whether they look behind or before them, to this world or the next, fear and trouble is their lot. Yea, many serious Christians, through the weakness of their trust in God, live in this perplexed strait, weary of living and afraid of dying, continually pressed between grief and fear. But Paul's strait was between two joys, which of them he should desire most. And if that be my case, what should much interrupt my peace or pleasure? If I live, it is for Christ, for his service, and to prepare for my own and his everlasting felicity: and should any suffering make me impatient with such a work, and such a life? If I die presently, it is my gain; God, who appoints me my work, limits my time; and surely his glorious reward can never be unseasonable, or come too soon, if it be the time that he appoints.

When I first engaged myself to preach the gospel, I reckoned as probable but upon one or two years, and God has made it above forty-four. And what reason have I to be unwilling now, either to live or die? God's service has been so sweet to me that it hath overcome the trouble of constant pains or weakness of the flesh, and all that men have said and done against me. How much the following crown exceeds this pleasure, I am not now able to conceive. There is some trouble in all this pleasant work, from which the soul and flesh would rest. And 'blessed are the dead which die in the Lord: Yea, saith the Spirit, that they may rest from their labours; and their works do follow them.' O my soul, what need has this kind of strait to trouble thee? Leave God to his own work, and mind that which is thine. So live that thou mayest say, 'Christ liveth in me; and the life which I now live in the flesh, I live by the faith of the Son of God, who loved me, and gave himself for me.' Then, as thou hast lived in the comfort of hope, thou shalt die in the comfort of vision and enjoyment. And when thou canst say of God, 'Whose I am, and whom I serve', thou mayest boldly add, 'I know whom I have believed, and into his hands I commit my departing spirit.'

2

THE SOULS OF THE GODLY ARE WITH CHRIST

The subject suggests to my thoughts the necessity of believing that the souls of the godly, when departed hence, shall be with Christ; and the reasonableness of such a faith. We are elsewhere assured that 'we shall be with him, where he is'. And to be with him can mean no less than a state of communion, and a participation of happiness. To believe such a state of happiness for departed pious souls, must appear upon consideration to be both necessary and reasonable.

1. The *necessity* of believing that pious separate spirits are with Christ appears by considering that without this belief (i) We shall be uncertain concerning the design of life; (ii) We shall lose the most powerful motive to a holy life; (iii) We can neither know, estimate, nor improve our mercies; (iv) Nor can we bear our suffering with comfort.

i. *We shall be uncertain concerning the design of life.* It is allowed that the right end of life is to please God. But I must desire to please God better than I do in this imperfect state, I must desire to please him perfectly. And our desires of our most ultimate end must have no bounds. God has made the desire of our own happiness so necessary to the soul of man, that it cannot be separated from our desire to please him. Therefore, both in respect to God, and to our own happiness, 'We must believe that he is the everlasting Rewarder of them that diligently seek him.' If we know not whether God will turn our pleasing him to our loss, or to our having no gain by pleasing him, this would hinder our love to him, and our trust and joy in him; and consequently hinder the cheerfulness, sincerity, and constancy of our obedience. Had we no certainty what God will do with us, we must have some probability and hope, before we can be entirely devoted to his service. How can a man pitch upon an uncertain end? If he waver so as to have no end, he can use no means; he lives not as a man, but as a brute. Of if he pitch upon a wrong end, he will but make work for repentance.

ii. *We shall lose the most powerful motives to a holy life.* Indeed, goodness is desirable for itself; but the goodness of means is their fitness for the end. We have here abundance of hindrances, temptations, and difficulties which must be overcome. Our natures are diseased, and greatly indisposed to the most necessary duties; and will they ever be discharged, if the necessary motives be not believed? Our duties to God and man may cost us our estates, liberties, and lives. The world is not so happy as commonly to know good men from bad, or to encourage piety and virtue, or to forbear opposing them. And who will let go his present welfare, without some hope of better as a reward? Men do not usually 'serve God for nought'; or while they think it will be their loss to serve him. A life of sin will not be avoided for inferior motives. When lust and appetite incline men strongly and constantly to their respective objects, what shall sufficiently restrain them, except the motives from things eternal? If sin so overspread the earth, notwithstanding all the hopes and fears of a life to come, what would it do if there were no such hopes and fears?

iii. *We can neither know, estimate, nor improve our mercies.* God gives us all the mercies of this life as helps to an immortal state of glory, and as earnests of it. Sensualists know not what a soul is, nor what soul mercies are, and therefore know not the just value of all bodily mercies, but take up only with the carcase, shell, or shadow, instead of the life of their mercies. No wonder they are so unthankful for God's mercies, when they know not the real excellency of them.

iv. *Nor can we bear our present sufferings with comfort, without the hopes of living with Christ.* What should support and comfort me under my bodily languishings and pains, my weary hours, and daily experience of the vanity and vexation of all things under the sun, had I not a prospect of the comfortable end of all? I that have lived in the midst of great and precious mercies have all my life had something to do to overcome the temptation of wishing that I had never been born; and had never overcome it, but by the belief of a blessed life hereafter. We should be strongly tempted, in our considerate moments, to murmur at our Creator, as dealing worse by us than by the brutes if we must have had all those cares and griefs and fears by the knowledge of what we lack, and the prospect of death and future evils, which they are exempted from, and had not withal the hopes of future felicity to support us.

Seneca had no better argument to silence such murmurings than to tell them, 'If this life have more evil than good, and you think God does you wrong, you may remedy yourselves, by ending it when you will.' But that could not cure the repinings of nature, when weary of the miseries of life, and yet afraid of dying. No wonder that so many fancied that souls were punished in these bodies for something done in a pre-existent state. 'O how contemptible a thing is man,' says Seneca, 'unless he lifts up himself above human things.' Therefore, says Solomon, when he had tried all sensual enjoyments, 'I hated life, because the work that is wrought under the sun is grievous unto me; for all is vanity and vexation of spirit.'

2. As for the *reasonableness* of believing that pious separate spirits are with Christ, I have often wondered

whether an implicit belief of it may not be better than searching into its nature, and trying what can be said against it. I have known many godly women who never disputed the matter but served God comfortably to a very old age, and who lived many years in such a cheerful readiness and desire for death as few studious men ever attain to. This, no doubt, was the divine reward of their long and faithful service of God, and trusting in him.

On the contrary, as doubts and difficulties are apt to present themselves to an inquisitive mind, they must be answered; for if we reject them unanswered, we give them half the victory over us; and a faith that is not upheld by such evidence of truth as reason can discern and justify, is often joined with much doubting, which men dare not open, but do not therefore overcome; and the weakness of such a faith may tend to enfeeble all the graces and duties which should be strengthened by it. Who knows how soon a temptation from Satan, or infidels, or from our own dark hearts, may assault us, which will not be overcome without clear evidence? Yet many that try, and reason, and dispute most, have not the stronger faith. Indeed, there is a wide difference between that light which discovers the thing itself, and a mere artificial kind of knowledge, to form arguments and answer objections.

Unlearned persons who have little of the latter may have more of the former, even that teaching from God, which reaches the heart, as well as the understanding. And who does not find it necessary to pray hard for this divine teaching? When I can prove the truth of the Word of God, and of the life to come, with the most convincing evidence of reason, I feel my need to cry daily to God, to 'increase my faith' and to give me that light which may sanctify the soul, and reach the end.

Nevertheless, this effectual teaching ordinarily supposes that which is artificial. Unlearned Christians are convinced, by good evidence, that God's Word is true, and his rewards sure; though they cannot state that evidence, or conceive of it without some confusion. With respect to curious and needless inquiries, beyond what is revealed, it is a believer's wisdom implicitly to trust his soul to Christ, and to fear that vain, vexatious knowledge which is selfish and savours of a distrust of God, and is that sin, and fruit of sin, which the learned world too little fears.

That 'God is the rewarder of them that diligently seek him', and that holy souls shall be in blessedness with Christ, I am convinced by the following concurrent evidences, on which my soul raises is hopes: The immortality of the soul; the belief of it naturally implanted in all men; the duty of all men to seek after future happiness; the difference between men and brutes, concerning the knowledge of God and futurity; the justice of God, as the Governor of the world; Divine revelation; God's hearing and answering prayer; the ministration of angels; the temptations of Satan; and, especially, the sanctifying operations of the Spirit of God.

i. *The soul of man is immortal, and, therefore, if good, cannot be for ever in a bad condition.* An immortal spirit is a distinct, self-conscious, invisible being, endowed with natural powers of never-ceasing action, understanding, and will, and which is neither annihilated nor destroyed by separation of parts. Such is the soul of man.

If in this flesh our spirits are not inactive and useless, we have no reason to think that they will be so hereafter, and that for ever. Though by the light of nature we may know the immortality of souls, yet, without supernatural light we know not what manner of action they will have in their separate state. It satisfies me that God will not continue their noblest powers in vain; and how those powers shall be exercised is known to him; and this his Word tells us more than nature. All things considered, there is no reason to fear that souls shall lose their activity, though they change their manner of action: and so it is naturally certain that they are immortal. And if holy souls are so far immortal, their holiness must infer their happy immortality. The most just and holy God will certainly use those well whom he makes holy.

ii. *The belief of the soul's immortality is naturally implanted in all men.* Almost all pagan nations at this day, as well as the Mahometans [Muslims], believe it. As for the cannibals and savages, whose understandings are least improved, they are rather ignorant of it than disbelieve it. Though some philosophers denied it, they were every way inconsiderable. Many others were doubtful, but they only professed to lack certainty, not probability. Most of the apostates from Christianity, besides those philosophers who have been its violent opposers, fully acknowledged it. Julian was so persuaded of it that, with a view to it, he exhorted his priests and the rest of his subjects to great strictness of life, and to see that the Christians did not exceed them. Indeed, few of those that affect, like the Sadducees, to disbelieve it, are able to free themselves from the fears of future misery; but with all their efforts, conscience still troubles them. And whence should all this be in man, and not in beasts, if man had no more cause for hopes and fears than they?

iii. *God has made it every man's duty to seek after future happiness, as the one thing needful, and therefore there must certainly be such a happiness for them that truly seek it.* Some believe a state of future retribution, as Christians, Mahometans, and most heathens. Others think it is uncertain, yet very probable. And to others it is also uncertain, though they rather think it untrue. Now all these ought to seek after it, and make it their chief care and labour; for natural reason requires every man to seek that which is best with the greatest diligence, and assures us that a probability or possibility of future everlasting happiness is better, and more worthy to be sought, than any thing attainable in this present life. As the will of man necessarily desires happiness, it must desire that most which is best and which is known to be so.

In this life there is nothing certain for an hour. It is certain that the longest life is short. It is certain that time and sensual pleasure, when past, are nothing, and no better than if they had never been. It is also certain that they are dissatisfying while we possess them; for carnal pleasure is no sweeter to a man than to a beast, and to a beast is unattended with fear of death, or any misery after death; nor has the beast any labours, sufferings, or trials, in order to obtain a future happiness, or avoid a future misery.

Besides, it is self-evident, from the perfections of God, and from the nature of his works, that he does not make it man's natural duty to care and labour most for that which is not, or to seek what is not to be attained. If so, the duty of man would result from deceit and falsehood; and God would govern the world by a lie, and not by power, wisdom, and love; and the better any man was, and the more he did his duty, he would be only the more deluded and miserable; and the more wicked and unbelieving any man was, the wiser and happier would he be. But all this is contrary to the perfections and works of God; for he makes nothing in vain, nor can he lie: much less will he make holiness itself, and all that duty and work of life which reason obliges all men to perform to be not only vain but pernicious.

iv. *The difference between men and beasts with respect to the knowledge of God and futurity shows that they differ as much in their hopes.* Man knows that there is a God by his works; and that this God is our Lord, our Ruler and end; and that we naturally owe him all our love and obedience; and that it is not the manner, even of good men, ever to suffer their most faithful servants to be losers by their fidelity, or to set them upon labouring in vain. Man also knows that his own soul is immortal, and therefore must be well or ill for ever, and that this ought to be cared for. And why should God give man all this knowledge more than to the brutes, if man is designed for no more happiness than brutes? Every wise man makes his work fit for its design: and will not God do so? If God was not perfectly wise, he would not be God. Therefore to deny man's future hopes, is to deny God himself.

v. *The justice of God as the Governor of the world infers a state of future retribution.* If God did not govern man by laws, judgment, and executions, there would be no proper law of nature, and man would have no proper duty, nor be in sin or fault. But experience tells us that God morally governs the world; and his right to do so is unquestionable.

If God was not the ruler of the world, the world would have no universal laws; for no man is the universal ruler; nor are kings, and other supreme powers, utterly lawless and ungoverned. And if God be a Ruler, he is just; else he is not so good as he requires earthly princes to be. But how is God a righteous Ruler, if he draws all men to himself by deceit; if he obliges them to seek and expect a reward which he will never give; if he makes man's duty his misery; if he requires man to labour in vain; if he suffer the wicked to persecute and kill his servants, without punishing the one, and gloriously recompensing the other in a future state?

vi. *The gospel revelation is the clear foundation of our faith and hope.* God has not left us to the mere light of nature. 'Christ has brought life and immortality to light.' One greater than an angel was sent from heaven to tell us what is there, and which is the way, and to secure our hopes. He has conquered death, and entered before us, as our Captain and Forerunner, into the everlasting habitations. He has 'all power in heaven and earth', and 'all judgment is committed to him'. All his Word is full of promises of our future glory at the resurrection.

Nor are we without assurance that the departing soul at death enters upon a state of joy and blessedness, as appears by the promise to the penitent thief on the cross; the parable of the rich man and Lazarus; Christ telling the Sadducees that God 'is not the God of the dead, but of the living'; the translation of Enoch and Elijah, and the appearance of Moses with Elijah on the mount of transfiguration; our Lord's arguing, that 'they who kill the body, are not able to kill the soul'; his 'commending his spirit into his Father's hands', and its being in paradise while his body was in the grave; his promising, 'Where I am, there shall also my servant be', etc.; Stephen's seeing heaven opened, and his praying, 'Lord Jesus, receive my spirit'; our being 'come to the spirits of just men made perfect'; Paul's desiring to depart, and to be with Christ, which is far better, and to be absent from the body, and present with the Lord; the blessedness of the dead which die in the Lord; the disobedient spirits being in prison, and the cities of Sodom and Gomorrah suffering the vengeance of eternal fire; also Christ's saying, 'When ye fail, (that is, leave this world) ye shall be received into everlasting habitations.'

vii. *God's hearing and answering prayer in this life assures his servants that he is their true and faithful Saviour.* How often have I cried to him when there appeared to be no help in second causes; and how frequently, suddenly, and mercifully, has he delivered me! Such extraordinary changes, beyond my own and others' expectations, while many plain-hearted, upright Christians, by fasting and prayer, sought God on my behalf, have abundantly convinced me of a special providence, and that God is indeed a hearer of prayer.

I have also seen wonders done for others by prayer more than for myself, though I and others are too much like those who 'cried unto the Lord in their trouble, and he saved them out of their distresses; but they forgot his works, and his wonders that he showed them'. And what were all those merciful answers but the fruits of Christ's power, faithfulness, and love, the fulfilling of his promises, and the earnest of the greater blessing of immortality, which the same promises entitle me to?

viii. *The ministration of angels is also a help to my belief of immortality with Christ.* They have charge over us, encamp round about us, bear us up in their hands, joy in the presence of God over our repentance, and are all ministering spirits, sent forth to minister to the heirs of salvation. As our angels, they always behold the face of our Father which is in heaven. When the Son of man shall come in his glory, all the holy angels shall come with him, and he shall send them forth, and they shall sever the wicked from among the just.

Not only of old did they appear to the faithful as messengers from God, but many mercies does God give to us by their ministry. And that they are now so friendly and helpful to us, and make up one society with us, greatly encourages us to hope that we are made for the same region, employment, and converse. They were once in a life of trial, though not on earth; and having overcome, they rejoice in our victory. The world above us is not uninhabited, nor beyond our capacity and hope; but we are come to the city of the living God, and to an innumerable company of angels.

ix. *Even Satan himself by his temptations has many ways cherished my hopes of immortality.* There are few men, I think, that observe what passes within them but have had some experience of such inward temptations as show that the author of them is an invisible enemy, and assure us that there are diabolical spirits which seek man's misery by tempting him to sin; and consequently that a future happiness or misery must be expected by us all.

x. *More especially the sanctifying operations of the Spirit of God are the earnest of heaven, and the sure prognostic of our immortal happiness.* It is a change of grand importance to man to be renewed in his mind, his will, and life. It repairs his depraved faculties. It causes man to live as man who was degenerated to a life too much like the brutes.

Men are slaves to sin, till Christ makes them free. 'Where the Spirit of the Lord is, there is liberty.' If 'the love of God shed abroad in our hearts' be not our excellence, health, and beauty, what is? 'That which is born of the flesh is flesh, and that which is born of the Spirit is spirit. 'Without Christ' and his Spirit 'we can do nothing'. Our dead notions and reason, though we see the truth, have not power to overcome temptations, nor raise up man's soul to its original and end, nor possess us with the love and joyful hopes of future blessedness. It were better for us to have no souls, than have our souls void of the Spirit of God. Heaven is the design and end of this important change.

What is our knowledge and faith, but to know and believe that heaven consists in the glory and love of God there manifested, and that it was purchased by Christ, and given by his covenant? What is our hope but 'the hope of glory', which we through the Spirit wait for? What is our love but a desire of communion with the blessed God, begun here, and perfected hereafter? What Christ teaches and commands, he works in us by his Spirit. He sends not his Spirit to make men craftier than others for this world, but 'wiser to salvation' and more holy and heavenly. 'The children of this world are in their generation wiser than the children of light.' Heavenly-mindedness is the special work of the Spirit. In producing this change, the Spirit overcomes all opposition from the world, the flesh, and the devil. Christ first overcame the world, and teaches and causes us to overcome it, even in its flatteries and its frowns. 'Our faith is our victory.' Whether this victory be easy and honourable to the Spirit of Christ, let us appeal to our experience of the wickedness of the world, and of our own weakness and falls.

None can do this work on the soul of man but God: not the most learned and holy teachers, or the wisest and most affectionate parents, or the greatest princes. Evil angels neither can nor will do it. Good angels do nothing toward it, but as obedient ministers of God. We cannot quicken, illuminate, or sanctify ourselves; and though we have some power, both conscience and experience testify that we have nothing but 'what we have received'. Christ promised his Spirit to all true believers, to be in them as his Advocate, Agent, Seal, and Mark; and indeed the Spirit here, and heaven hereafter, are the chief of his promises.

That this Spirit is given to all true believers is evident by the effects of his being given. They have ends, affections, and lives different from the rest of mankind; they live upon the hopes of a better life, and their heavenly interest overrules all the opposite interests of this world. In order to this they live under the conduct of divine authority, and to obey and please God is the great business of their lives. The men of the world discern this difference, and therefore hate and oppose them, because they find themselves condemned by their heavenly temper and conversation. Believers are conscious of this difference; for they desire to be better, and to trust and love God more, and to have more of the heavenly life and comforts; and when their infirmities make them doubt of their own sincerity, they would not change their Governor, rule, or hopes, for all the world; and it is never so well and pleasant with them, as when they can trust and love God most; and in their worst and weakest condition they would fain be perfect.

Indeed, whatever real goodness is found among men, it is given by the same Spirit of Christ. But it is notorious that, in heavenly-mindedness and virtue, no part of the world is comparable to serious Christians.

This Spirit Christ also expressly promised, as the means and pledges, the first-fruits and earnest, of the heavenly glory; and therefore it is a certain proof that we shall have such a glory. He that gives us a spiritual change which in its nature and tendency is heavenly; he that sets our hopes and hearts on heaven, and turns the endeavours of our lives towards future blessedness; he that promised this preparatory grace as the earnest of that felicity, may well be trusted to perform his Word in our complete eternal glory.

3. And now, O weak and fearful soul, why shouldest thou draw back, as if the matter was *doubtful*? Is not thy foundation firm? Is not the way of life, through the valley of death, made safe by him that conquered death? Art thou not yet delivered from the bondage of thy fears?

Hast thou not long ago found in thee the motions and effectual operations of this Spirit? And is he not still residing and working in thee, as the Agent and Witness of Christ?

If not, whence are thy groanings after God, thy desires to be nearer to his glory, to know him and love him more? Whence came all the pleasure thou hast had in his sacred truth, and ways, and service? Who subdued for thee thy folly, pride, and vain desires? Who made it thy choice to sit at the feet of Jesus, and hear his Word, as the better part, and count the honours and preferments of the world but dung and dross? Who breathed in thee all those requests thou hast sent up to God? Overvalue not corrupt nature – it brings forth no such fruits as these. Remember what thou wast in the hour of temptation, how small a matter has drawn thee to sin. Forget not the days of thy youthful vanity. Overlook not the case of thy sinful neighbours, who, in the midst of light still live in darkness, and hear not the loudest calls of God. Is it no work of Christ's Spirit that has made thee to differ? Thou hast nothing to boast of, and much to be humbled and also to be thankful for.

Thy holy desires are, alas! too weak; but they are holy. Thy love has been too cold; but it is the most holy God whom thou hast loved. Thy hopes have been too low; but thou hast hoped in God, and for his heavenly glory. Thy prayers have been too dull and interrupted; but thou hast prayed for holiness and heaven. Thy labours have been too slothful; but thou hast laboured for God and Christ, and the good of mankind. Though thy motion was too weak and slow, it has been God-ward, and therefore it is from God. O bless the Lord, not only for giving thee his Word, and sealing it with uncontrolled miracles, but also for frequently and remarkably fulfilling his promises, in the answer of thy prayers, and in great deliverance of thyself and of many others; and that he has by regeneration been preparing thee for the light of glory! And wilt thou yet doubt and fear, against all this evidence, experience, and foretaste?

4. I think it no needless labour to confirm my soul in the *full persuasion* of the truth of its immortal nature, and of a future life of joy or misery, and of the certain truth of the Christian faith. I can no more doubt the being and perfections of God than whether there be an earth or a sun. Christianity is only known by revelation, which is so attested externally to the world and internally to holy souls as to make faith a ruling victorious, and comfortable principle. But the soul's immortality and future reward is known in some measure by the light of nature, and more perfectly by revelation.

When I consider the great unlikeliness of men's hearts and lives to such a belief as we all profess, I cannot but fear, that not only the ungodly, but most that truly hope for glory, have a far weaker belief of the soul's immortality, and the truth of the gospel, than they are apt to imagine. Can I be fully persuaded of the future rewards and punishments of souls, and that we shall be judged hereafter as we have lived here, without despising all the vanities of the world, and setting my heart with resolution and diligence to a holy, heavenly, fruitful life? Who could stand trifling as most men do at the door of eternity, that verily believed his immortal soul must be shortly there? Though such a one had no certainty of his own salvation, he would nevertheless search and try, watch and pray, and spare no care, cost, or labour, to make all sure. If a man once saw heaven and hell, would he not afterwards exceed the most resolute believer? I confess there is much weakness of faith in things unseen, even where there is sincerity. But where there is little diligence for the world to come, I must think there is but little belief of it, and that such persons are not aware how much they secretly doubt the truth of it. Most complain of the uncertainty of their title to salvation, and very little of their uncertainty of a heaven and a hell, whereas a hearty persuasion of the latter would do more to convince them of the former than long examinations and many marks of trial.

It would indeed confound faith and reason if in the body we had as clear and lively apprehensions of heaven and hell as sight would occasion; nor is the soul fit, while in the body, to bear such a sight. But yet there is an over-ruling seriousness to which the soul must be brought by a firm persuasion of future things. And he that is careful and serious for this world, and looks after a better only in the second place, must give me leave to think that he believes but as he lives, and that his doubting of a heaven and hell is greater than his belief.

5. O then, for what should my soul more pray, than for a *clearer and stronger faith*? 'I believe; Lord, help my unbelief!' I have many thousand times groaned to thee under this burden of remaining darkness and unbelief: I have many thousand times thought of the evidences of Christianity, and of the necessity of a lively, powerful, active faith. I have cried to thee night and day, 'Lord, increase my faith!' I have written and spoken that to others which might be more useful to myself, and render my faith more like sense. Yet, Lord, how dark is this world! What a dungeon is flesh! How little clearer are my perceptions of things unseen, than they were long ago! Is no more growth of them to be expected? Does the soul no more increase in vigorous perception, when the body no more increases in the vigour of sensation? Must I sit down with so low a measure, when I am almost there, where faith is changed for sight?

O let not a soul, that is driven from this world, and weary of vanity, and can think of little else but immortality, that seeks and cries both night and day for the heavenly light, and fain would have some foretaste of glory, and some more of the first-fruits of the promised joys, let not such a soul either long, or cry, or strive in vain! Punish not my former grieving of thy Spirit by deserting a soul that cries for thy grace, so near its great and inconceivable change! Let me not languish in vain desires at the door of hope; nor pass with doubts and fears from this vale of misery! Which should be the season of triumphant faith and hope and joy if not when I am entering on the world of joy? O thou that has left us so many words of promise 'that our joy may be full', send, O send the Comforter, for without his heavenly beams, after a thousand thoughts and cares, it will still be night and winter with my soul!

7. But I fear a *distrust* of God and my Redeemer has had too great a hand in my desires after a more distinct knowledge than God ordinarily gives to souls in flesh. I know that I should implicitly, absolutely, and quietly commit my soul into my Redeemer's hands; for a distrustful care of the soul, as well as the body, is our great sin and misery.

Yet we must desire that our knowledge and belief may be as distinct as divine revelations are. We can love no farther than we know; and the more we know of God and glory, the more we shall love, desire, and trust.

If I may not be ambitious of too sensible and distinct foretastes of things unseen, yet I must desire and beg the most fervent love of them that I am capable of, that my soul may not pass with distrust and terror, but with suitable triumphant hopes, to everlasting pleasures.

O Father of lights, who givest wisdom to them that ask, shut not up this sinful soul in darkness! Leave me not to grope in unsatisfied doubts, at the door of celestial light! Deny me not now the lively exercise of faith, hope, and love, which are the stirrings of the new creature, the dawnings of eternal day, and the earnest of the promised inheritance!

Though, like Cicero after reading Plato's book on immortality, our doubts return, and our fear interrupts and weakens our desires and joys, yet I find that it is chiefly an irrational fear, occasioned by the darkness of the mind, the greatness of the change, the dreadful majesty of God, and man's natural aversion to death, even when reason is fully satisfied that such fear is consistent with certain safety.

Were I on the top of a castle or steeple, fastened by the strongest chains, or guarded by the surest battlements, I could not possibly look down without fear; and so it is with our prospect into the life to come. If, therefore, my soul sees undeniable evidence of immortality, and is able by irrefragable arguments to prove a future blessedness; if I am convinced that divine promises are true, and trust my soul, and all my hope, upon them; then neither my averseness to dying nor my irrational fear of entering upon eternity can invalidate the reasons of my hope or prove the unsoundness of my faith, but only the weakness of it.

'Why are ye fearful, O ye of little faith?', was Christ's reproof to his disciples. A timorous heart needs to be chided, by saying, 'Why art thou cast down, O my soul? And why art thou disquieted within me? hope in God: for I shall yet praise him, who is the health of my countenance, and my God.'

3

DEPARTING TO BE WITH CHRIST

Having proved that faith and hope have a certain future happiness to expect, the text directs me next to consider, *What it is to be with Christ;* and, *What it is to depart in order to be with him.*

1. To be with *Christ includes presence with him, union to him, and participation of his happiness.*

i. *The presence of Christ* which pious separate spirits shall enjoy must refer to his Godhead, as well as to his human soul and body. We shall be present with the divine nature of Christ, as manifested in and by his glory. He teaches us to pray, 'Our Father, which art in heaven,' because in heaven the Father gloriously shines forth to holy souls. The soul of man is eminently said to be in the head, because there it understands and reasons; and not in the foot or hand, though it be also there. As we look a man in the face when we talk to him, so we look up to heaven when we pray to God. Though 'in God we live, and move, and have our being,' both as the God of nature and grace, yet by the works and splendour of his glory he is eminently in heaven, manifesting himself there by some created glory; for his essence is the same everywhere.

We shall be present with the human nature of Christ, both soul and body. But here our present narrow thoughts must not too boldly presume to determine the difference between Christ's glorified body, and his flesh upon earth; nor where his glorified body is, nor how far it extends; nor wherein his soul and his glorified body differ, seeing it is called a spiritual body. We can conceive no more of such a body than that it is pure, incorruptible, invisible to mortal eyes, and fitted to the most perfect state of the soul. Nor need we wonder how a whole world of glorified bodies can all of them be present with the one body of Christ; for as the solar beams are so present with the air that none can discern the difference of the places which they possess, and a world of bodies are present with them both, so may all our bodies, without any confusion, be present with Christ's body.

ii. The *union to Christ*, which pious separate spirits shall also enjoy, must be like that of subjects to their king, but how much more we know not. The more spiritual, pure and noble any natures are, the more inclination they have to union. Such instances of union as the vine and branches, the head and members, are of extensive import; yet these being but similitudes, we cannot determine how extensive. Far be it from us to think that Christ's glorified body is of such an earthly composition and of such a limited extent as it was here; for then, as his disciples and a few more were present with him, while the rest of the world were absent and had none of his company, so it would be in heaven. But all true believers from the creation to the end of the world, as well as Paul, shall 'be with Christ, and see his glory'. And though there will be different degrees of glory, as there have been of holiness, yet none in heaven are at such a distance from Christ as not to enjoy the felicity of his presence.

iii. We shall also have *communion with the divine and human natures of Christ;* both which shall be the felicitating objects of perfect knowledge and holy love to the separate spirits, before the resurrection. The chief part of this communion will consist in Christ's communications to the soul. As the whole creation is more dependent on God than the fruit on the tree, or the plant on the earth, or the members on the body, so God uses second causes in his communications to inferior natures; and it is more than probable, that Christ's human nature is the second cause of communicating both grace and glory, both to man in the body and to the separate soul.

As the sun is both the cause and object of sight to the eye, so is Christ to the soul. For as God, so the Lamb is the light and glory of the heavenly Jerusalem, and in his light they shall have light. Though Christ shall give up the kingdom to the Father, so that God may be 'all in all,' and his creatures be fully restored to his favour, and a healing government for recovering lapsed souls to God shall be no more needed; yet surely he will not cease to be our Mediator, the church's Head, and the channel of everlasting light, life, and love to all his members.

As 'we now live, because he lives', like the branches in the vine; and as the Spirit that now quickens, enlightens, and sanctifies us is first the Spirit of Christ before he is ours, and is communicated from God through him to us, so will it be in the state of glory. There our union and communion with him will be perfected, and not destroyed or diminished. As it would be arrogance to think we shall be above the need and use of Christ and his communications, so, I doubt not, we shall ever have use for one another, as is plainly intimated by 'sitting down with Abraham, Isaac, and Jacob, in the kingdom of God'; by being 'in Abraham's bosom'; by 'sitting at Christ's right and left hand in his kingdom'; by being 'made ruler over ten cities'; and by joining with those that 'sing the song of Moses and of the Lamb'.

And certainly if I be 'with Christ' I shall be with all them that are with Christ, even with all the heavenly society. Our mortal bodies must have so much room that the earth is little enough for all its inhabitants. So narrow is our capacity of communion here that those of the antipodes, or on the opposite side of the earth, are almost as strange to us as if they were in another world. What strangers we are to those of another kingdom, county, or parish, and even of another house! But we have great cause to think, by many scriptural expressions, that our heavenly union and communion will be nearer and more extensive, and that all the glorified shall know each other.

It is, I confess, a pleasant thought to me, and greatly helps my willingness to die, to think that I shall go to all the holy ones, both Christ and angels and pious separate spirits. They are each of them better and more amiable than I am. Many are better than one, and the perfect whole than a sinful part, and the New Jerusalem is the glory of the creation. God has given me a love to all that are holy, for their holiness; and a love to the work of love and praise, which they continually and perfectly perform; and a love to his celestial habitation, to his glory shining there. My old acquaintance with many a holy person gone to Christ makes my thoughts of heaven the more familiar to me. O how many of them could I name! And it is no small encouragement to one that is to enter upon an unseen world to think that he goes no untrodden path, nor enters into a solitary or singular state, but follows all that have passed by death, from the creation to this day, into endless life. O how emboldening to consider, that I am to go the same way and to the same place and state as all the believers and saints that have ever gone before me!

2. *But I must depart, before I can thus be with Christ.* I must particularly depart from this body, from all its former delights, and also from more rational pleasures belonging to the present life and world.

i. *I must depart from this body*. Here these eyes must see no more, this hand move no more, these feet walk no more, this tongue speak no more. As much as I have loved – and over-loved – this body, I must leave it to the grave. There must it lie and rot in darkness, as a neglected and loathsome thing. This is the fruit of sin, and nature would not have it so. But it is only my shell, my tabernacle, my clothing, and not my soul itself. It is only a dissolution; earth to earth, water to water, air to air, and fire to fire. It is but an instrument laid by, when all its work is done; a servant dismissed, when his service is ended; as I cast by my lute when I have better employment. It is but as flowers die in autumn, and plants in winter. It is but a separation from a troublesome companion, and putting off a shoe that pinched me.

Many a sad and painful hour, many a weary night and day have I had. What cares and fears, what griefs and groans has this body cost me! Alas! how much of my precious time has been spent to maintain, please, or repair it! Often have I thought that it cost me so dear to live, yea, to live a painful weary life, that were it not for the higher ends of life, I had little reason to be much in love with it, or be loath to leave it.

To depart from such a body, is but to remove from a sordid habitation. I know it is the curious, wonderful work of God, and not to be despised or unjustly dishonoured but admired and well used; yet our reason wonders that so noble a spirit should be so meanly housed, for we must call it 'our vile body'. To depart from such a body is but to be loosed 'from the bondage of corruption', from the clog and prison of the soul. That body which was a fit servant to the soul of innocent man is now become as a prison. And further, to depart from such a body is but to be separated from an accidental enemy, and one of our greatest and most hurtful enemies; not, indeed, as the work of our Creator, but as the effect of sin. What could Satan, or any other enemy of our souls, have done against us without our flesh? What is it but the interest of this body that stands in competition with the interest of God and our souls? What else do the profane sell their heavenly inheritance for, as Esau his birthright? What else is the bait of ambition, covetousness, and sensuality? What takes up the thoughts and cares which we should lay out upon things spiritual and heavenly, but this body and its life? What steals away men's hearts from the heavenly pleasures of faith, hope, and love, but the pleasures of this flesh? This draws us to sin, and hinders us from and in our duty.

Were it not for bodily interest and its temptations, how much more innocent and holy might I live! I should have nothing to care for, but to please God and be pleased in him, were it not for the care of this bodily life. What employment should my will and love have but to delight in God and love him and his interest, were it not for the love of the body, and its concerns? By this our mind is darkened, our thoughts diverted, our wills corrupted, our heart and time alienated from God, our guilt increased, our heavenly desires and hopes destroyed; life is made unholy and uncomfortable and death terrible; God and souls are separated, and eternal life is neglected and in danger of being utterly lost. I know that in all this the sinful soul is the chief cause and agent – but is not bodily interest its temptation, bait, and end? Is not the body, and its life and pleasure, the chief alluring cause of all this sin and misery? And shall I take such a body to be better than heaven, or refuse to be loosed from so troublesome a yoke-fellow, and separated from so burdensome and dangerous a companion?

ii. *I must depart from all the former pleasures of this body*. I must taste no more sweetness in meat or drink, in rest or action, or any such thing as now delights me. Houses and lands, goods and wealth, must all be left; and the place where I live must know me no more. All I laboured for, or took delight in, must be no more to me than if they had never been.

But consider, O my soul! Thy former pleasures are already past. Thou losest none of them by death, for they are all lost before; unless immortal grace has made them immortal by sanctifying them. All that death does to me is to prevent the repetition of them upon earth. Is not the pleasure which we lose by death common to every brute? Meat is as sweet to them, and ease as welcome, and appetite as vehement. Why then should it seem hard to us to lose that, when God pleases, which we deprive the brutes of at our pleasure? If we are believers, we only exchange these delights of life for the greater delights of a life with

Christ; a comfort which our fellow-creatures the brutes have not. Are not the pleasures of life usually embittered with such pain that they seldom countervail the attending vanity and vexation? It is true nature desires life under sufferings that are tolerable rather than die. But that is not so much from the sensible pleasure of life as from mere natural inclination to life which God has implanted in us.

Do we not willingly interrupt these pleasures every night, when we betake ourselves to sleep? To say that rest is my pleasure is but to say that my daily labours and cares are so much greater than my waking pleasures that I am glad to lay by both together. If we can thus be content every night to die, as it were, to all our waking pleasures, why should we be unwilling to die to them at once? If they be forbidden pleasures which you are unwilling to leave, those must be left before you die; otherwise you had better never have been born. Every wise and godly man casts them off with detestation. Indeed, the same cause which makes men unwilling to live a holy life has a great hand in making them unwilling to die – even because they are loth to leave the pleasures of sin.

If the wicked be converted, he must be gluttonous and drunken no more; he must live in pride, vanity, worldly-mindedness and sensual pleasures no more; and therefore he draws back from a holy life as it were from death itself. But what is this to those who 'have mortified the flesh, with the affections and lusts'? Consider also that these forbidden pleasures are the great impediments, both of our holiness and of our truest pleasures. One of the reasons why God forbids them is because they hinder us from better. And if for our own good we must forsake them when we turn to God, we should therefore be the more willing to die in order to be free from the danger of them; and especially since death will transmit us to infinitely greater pleasures.

iii. *I must also depart from the more rational pleasures which I have enjoyed in this body; as for instance, from my present studies*, which are delights far above those of sensual sinners.

But let me consider: how small is our knowledge compared with our ignorance! How little does the knowledge of the learned differ from the thoughts of a child! As trifles are the matter of childish knowledge, so artificial words and forms make up more of the learning of the world than is commonly understood. God and the life to come are little better known by the learned, and often much less, than by many of the unlearned. Of how little use is it to know what is contained in many hundred volumes that fill our libraries and have given their authors the name of *virtuosi* – not for their having the virtue to live to God, or overcome temptations from the flesh and the world and secure their everlasting hopes!

Much of our reading and learning, alas! does us more harm than good. Many a precious hour is lost in them that should be employed in higher pursuits. To many, I fear, it is as unholy a pleasure as others take in thinking of lands and honours; only the more dangerous for being the less suspected. I know the knowledge of natural things is valuable, and may be sanctified, and made some way useful to my highest ends, and I would be at any expense to procure more. But I must earnestly pray, 'May the Lord forgive me the hours that I have spent in reading things less profitable, for the sake of pleasing a mind that would fain know every thing, instead of spending them for the increase of holiness in myself and others.'

Yet I must thankfully acknowledge to God that from my youth he taught me to begin with things of the greatest weight, and to refer most of my other studies thereto, and to spend my days under the motives of necessity and profit to myself, and those that were committed to me. I would have men most relish that learning in their health, which they will find sweetest in sickness, and when near to death.

And, alas! how expensive a vanity is this knowledge! Though it little differs from a pleasant dream, yet, to attain a little excellency in it, how many laborious days and weeks must it cost us! 'Much study is a weariness of the flesh, and he that increaseth knowledge increaseth sorrow.' What painful diseases and loss of bodily ease and health has it occasioned me! What envy and opposition has it exposed me to! And should a man be loth to die for fear of leaving such troublesome, costly learning and knowledge? Let me especially consider that we shall certainly have a nobler, sweeter, and more extensive knowledge than is here attainable. Love never fails, and we can love no more than we know. But 'prophecies shall fail; tongues shall cease; knowledge', such as we now have, 'shall vanish away. When I was a child, I spake as a child, I understood as a child, I thought as a child; but when I became a man, I put away childish things. For now we see through a glass, darkly; but then face to face: now I know in part; but then shall I know even as also I am known'; for though my knowledge will not be like that of the blessed God, it will be like that of holy spirits.

In order for a physician to describe the disease of his patient, he needs much reading and close inquiry. And after all he goes much upon conjectures, and his knowledge is mixed with many uncertainties and mistakes; but when he opens his corpse, his knowledge is more full and true, and obtained with greater ease and speed. A countryman knows the town, fields, and rivers, plants, and animals where he dwells with ease, perspicuity, and certainty, when mere geographical knowledge is liable to many mistakes. So the sight of God and heaven will deserve the name of wisdom, while our present glimpse is but philosophy, or the love of wisdom.

We should not, therefore, fear death, for fear of losing our knowledge; but rather long for the world of glorious light, that we may get out of this darkness into easy, joyful and satisfying knowledge.

Friendship is one of the more rational pleasures enjoyed in this body and from which I must depart. He that believes not that there are far more and better friends in heaven than there are on earth believes not, as he ought, that there is a heaven. Our friends here are wise; but they are also unwise. They are faithful, but partly unfaithful. They are holy, but, alas! too sinful. They have the image of God; but it is blotted and dishonoured by their faults. They do God and his church much service; but they also do too much for Satan, even when they intend the honour of God. They promote the gospel; but they also hinder it by their weakness and ignorance, their selfishness, pride, and passion, divisions and contentions. They are our helpers and comforters; but how often are they also our hindrances, trouble and grief. In heaven they are perfectly wise and holy and faithful; and there is nothing in them nor done by them but what is amiable to God and man. With our faithful friends we have here a mixture of those that are useless and burdensome, or hypocritical and malicious.

But in heaven there are none but the wise and holy; no hypocrites, no burdensome neighbours, no treacherous, oppressive, or persecuting enemies. Christ loved his disciples, his kindred and all mankind, and took pleasure in doing good to all; and so did his apostles; but how poor a recompense had he or they from any, but from God! Christ's 'brethren believed not on him'. Peter denied him. 'All his disciples forsook him and fled.' And what then could be expected from others? No friends have a perfect suitableness to each other: and those inequalities that are nearest to us, are most troublesome. So various and contrary are our apprehensions, interests, education, our

[49]

tempers, inclinations, and temptations that, instead of wondering at the discord and confusions of the world, we may rather admire the providence of God, which maintains so much order and concord. The greatest crimes that have been charged upon me have been those things which I thought to be my greatest duties; and for those parts of my obedience to God and my conscience which cost me dearest, and where I pleased my flesh least, I pleased the world least. And is this tumultuous, militant world a place that I should be loth to leave?

I must depart from all *the means of grace*, though more precious to me than all earthly enjoyments. Shall I love the name of heaven better than heaven itself? Is not the possession of glory better than the promise of it? If a light and guide through the wilderness be good, surely the glorious end must be better.

It hath pleased God that all things on earth, even the sacred Scriptures, should bear the marks of our state of imperfection. Imperfect persons were the penmen. Imperfect human language is the conveyance. Heaven will not, to perfect spirits, be made the occasion of so many errors and controversies, as the Scriptures are to us imperfect mortals. Yea, heaven is the more desirable, because there I shall better understand the Scriptures than here I can ever hope to do.

To leave my Bible and to go to the God and heaven which the Bible reveals will be no otherwise my loss than to leave the picture for the presence of my friend. As for mere human writings and instructions, the pleasure of my mind is much abated by their great imperfection; and why should I think that my own are blameless? I must for ever be thankful for the holy instructions and writings of others, notwithstanding human frailty; and so must I be thankful that God hath made any use of my own for the good of souls and the edification of his church.

But how many alloys are there to such comforts! If good men and good books or sermons would make the world seem over-lovely, it will be the mercy of God to abate the temptation. When we are dead to the love of the godly themselves, of learning, books and ordinances, so far as they serve a selfish interest and tempt our hearts from heavenly aspirations, then indeed, 'the world is crucified to us, and we to it'.

Of all things, a departing soul has least cause to fear losing *the knowledge of worldly affairs*. If the sun gives light and heat to the earth, why should I think that blessed spirits have no acquaintance with earthly concerns? From the top of a hill I can see more than from below; and shall I know less of earth from heaven than I do now? It is un-likely that my capacity will be so little or that Christ and all the angels will be so strange to me as to give me no notice of things so interesting to my God and Redeemer, to the holy society of which I am a member, and to myself as a member of that society.

Spirits are most active and of quick and powerful com-munication. They need not send letters, nor write books, nor lift up a voice. And as activity, so unity is greatest where there is most perfection. Their knowledge, love and joy will be one. My celestial advancement, therefore, will be no diminution but an inconceivable increase of my desirable knowledge of things on earth. If, indeed, I shall know less of things below, it will be because the knowledge of them is a part of vanity and vexation which have no place in heaven. I need not be afraid to hear any more of bloody wars, desolated countries, dissipated churches, persecuted Christians, silenced preachers, party conflicts, contentious divines, censorious professors of religion, with the cries of the poor, or the endless complaints of the melancholy.

Nor need I fear, what other men are pleased to suggest, that *the church will want me*. Is it I, or God, that must choose his servants, and cut out their work? Am I doing God's work, or my own? If God's, must not he say what and when and how long? And will not his will and choice be best? If I believe not this, how do I take him for my God? Does God, or I, know best what is yet to be done, and who is fittest to do it?

What am I to those more excellent persons, whom in all ages God hath taken out of the world? Have not many servants of Christ died in their youth who were far more likely to win souls and glorify God than I am, or ever have been? And shall I, at seventy-six years of age, after such a life of unspeakable mercies, and after almost fifty-three years of comfortable help in the service of my Lord, be now afraid of my reward and shrink at the sentence of death, and still be desirous to stay here under pretence of farther service?

We know not what is best for the church as God does. The church and the world are not ours but his: not our desires, therefore, but his will must measure out its mercies. Nothing ever lay so heavy on my heart as the sin and misery of mankind, and to think how much of the world lies in folly and wickedness.

And for what can I so heartily pray as for the world's recovery? And it is his will that I should show a holy and universal love by praying, 'Let thy name be hallowed; thy kingdom come; thy will be done on earth, as it is in heaven.'

Yet, alas! how unlike is earth to heaven! What sin and ignorance, confusion and cruelties, reign and prosper here! Without a wonderful change, even by a general miracle, how little hope appears, that even these prayers should be answered! Indeed, it makes us better to desire that others may be better; and God seems to permit the ignorance and confusion of this world to help us the more to value and desire the world of light, love and order.

If I am any way useful to the world, undeserved mercy hath made me so, for which I must be thankful. How long I shall be so is not my business to determine but my Lord's. As God will be served and pleased by wonderful variety of animals and vegetables, so he will by their successive generations. If one flower fall or die, others in future summers shall arise from the same root. God will have other generations to succeed us; let us thank him that we have had our time.

And could we without selfishness love others as ourselves, and God as God, it would comfort us at death to have others survive us and the world continue and God still be God and be glorified in his works. Love would say, 'I shall live in my successors; I shall more than live in the life of the world; and most of all, in the eternal life and glory of God.' Nor will God try us with too long a life of temptations, lest we should grow too familiar where we should be strangers and be utterly strangers to our home.

No wonder the world was prepared for a deluge by a deluge of sin, when men lived six, seven, eight, or nine hundred years! Had our great sensualists any hope of living so long, they would be like incarnate devils; there would be no dwelling near them for the godly. Nor will God tire us with too long a life of afflictions. And shall we grudge at the wisdom and goodness which shortens them? Though holy duties be excellent and delightful, yet the weakness of the flesh makes us liable to weariness and abates the willingness of the spirit. By our weariness and complaints, our fears and groans, we seem to think this life too long; and yet when we should yield to the call of God, we draw back as if we would have it to be everlasting.

Willingly submit, then, O my soul! It is not thyself, but this flesh that must be dissolved; this troublesome, vile, and corruptible flesh. Study thy duty, work while it is day, and let God choose thy time; and willingly stand to his disposal.

When I die, the gospel dies not, the church dies not, the praises of God die not, the world dies not, but perhaps it will grow better, and those prayers be answered which seemed to be lost; and perhaps some of the seed I have sown will spring up when I am dead.

If my end was to do good and glorify God, when good is done and God is glorified, though I were annihilated, is not my end attained? 'Lord, let thy servant depart in peace'; even in thy peace, 'which passeth all understanding,' and which Christ, the Prince of peace, gives, and which nothing in the world can take away! O give me that peace, which suits a soul who is so near the harbour, even the world of endless peace and love! Call home this soul by the encouraging voice of love, that it may joyfully hear and say: It is my Father's voice!

Invite it to thee by the heavenly messenger. Attract it by the tokens and foretastes of love! The messengers that invited me to the feast of grace compelled me to come in without constraint; thy effectual call made me willing. And is not glory better than the grace which prepares for it? Shall I not more willingly come to the celestial feast? What was thy grace for, but to make me desirous of glory, and the way of it? Why didst thou dart down thy beams of love, but to make me love thee, to call me up to the everlasting centre? Was not the feast of grace as a sacrament of the feast of glory? Did I not take it in remembrance of my Lord till he come? Did not he that told me, 'All things are ready', tell me also, that 'He is gone to prepare a place for us', and that 'he will have us to be with him, and see his glory'? They that are given him and drawn to him by the Father on earth do come to Christ. Give now and draw my departing soul to my glorified Head! As I have glorified thee on earth, in the measure of thy grace bestowed upon me, pardon the sins by which I have offended thee, and glorify me in the vision and participation of my Redeemer's glory!

Come, Lord Jesus, come quickly, with fuller life and light and love, into this too dead and dark and disaffected soul, that with joyful willingness I may come unto thee!

Willingly depart, O lingering soul! It is from a Sodom. Though there be righteous Lots in it, they are not without their sad blemishes. Hast thou so often lamented the general blindness and wickedness of the world, and art thou loth to leave it for a better? How often wouldst thou have rejoiced to have seen but the dawning of a day of universal peace and reformation? And wouldst thou not see it, where it shines in perfect beauty? Hast thou prayed and laboured so hard to have the pleasure of a light at midnight; and is it not thy desire to behold the Sun itself? Will the things of heaven please thee nowhere but on earth, where they are least and weakest?

Away, away! Vindictive flames are ready to consume this sinful world. Sinners are treasuring up wrath against the day of wrath. Look not then behind thee. Away from this unhappy world! 'Press toward the mark; looking for, and hastening unto the coming of the day of God.' As this world hath used thee, it would still do so. When thou hast fared best in it, no thanks to it, but to God. If thou hast had manifold deliverances and preservations and hast been fed with angels' food, love not the wilderness, but thy heavenly Guide, Protector, and Deliverer. Does God in great mercy make pain and feebleness the harbingers of death, and wilt thou not understand their business? Wouldst thou dwell with thy beloved body in the grave, where it will rot in loathsome darkness? If not, why should it now, in its painful languor, seem to thee a more pleasing habitation than the glorious presence of thy Lord? In the grave it will be at rest, nor will it at night wish, 'O that it were morning', nor in the morning say, 'When will it be night?' And is this a dwelling fit for thy delight? Patience in it, while God will so try thee, is thy duty: but is such patience a better and sweeter life than rest and joy?

But, alas! how deaf is flesh to reason! I have reason enough to be willing to depart, even much more willing than I am. O that I could be as willing as reason convinces me I ought to be! Could I love God as much as I know I ought to love him, then I should desire to depart and to be with Christ as much as I know I ought to desire it. But death must be a penalty, even where it is a gain; and therefore it must meet with some unwillingness.

Because we willingly sinned, we must unwillingly suffer. All the faith and reason in the world will not make death to be no penalty, and therefore will not take away all unwillingness. No man ever reasoned or believed himself into a love of pain and death as such. But since the gain is unspeakably greater than the pain and loss, therefore faith and holy reason may make our willingness greater than our unwillingness, and our hope and joy greater than our fear and sorrow.

Come then, my soul, and think believingly what is best for thee; and wilt thou not love and desire that most which is certainly best?

4

WHY IT IS FAR BETTER TO BE WITH CHRIST

To say or hear that it is far better to be with Christ is not enough to make us willing. If I firmly believe that it is better for me, I shall then desire it. And have I not reason to believe it? Let me seriously consider for my full conviction: 1. *By what means I am preparing for this happiness;* 2. *How this happiness is the end for which I am preparing;* and 3. *How it will perfect my knowledge, will, and activity in doing good.*

1. *The means by which I am preparing to be with Christ abundantly show that it is far better to be with him:* as, for instance, *that which my heavenly Father's love designs and chooses for my good* is better for me. I hope I shall never dare to say or think that he is mistaken, or that I could have chosen better for myself. Many a time hath the wise and good will of God crossed my foolish,

rebellious will, and afterwards I have perceived it was best. It is not an enemy nor a tyrant that made me, preserves me, or calls me hence. The more I have tried him, the better I have found him. Had I better obeyed his ruling will, how happy had I been! And is not his disposing and rewarding will as good? Should I not die till myself or any of my dearest friends would have it so, would this rejoice me? O foolish, sinful soul, is it not far better to be at God's choice, than my own, or any man's?

Be of good cheer, then, O my soul! It is thy Father's voice that calls thee hence: his voice, that called thee into being, and out of a state of sin and death, and bade thee live unto him; that called thee so often from the grave, forgave thy sins, renewed thy strength, restored thee to the comforts of his house and service, and hath so graciously led thee through this howling wilderness, almost to the sight of the promised land. And wilt thou not willingly go, when such infinite love calls thee? Art thou not desirous of his presence? Art thou afraid to go to him, who is the only cure of thy fears? What was it but this glory, to which he elected thee? Not to the riches and honours of this world, or the pleasures of the flesh, but chose thee in Christ to an inheritance in glory? If God choose thee to blessedness, refuse it not thyself, nor behave like a refuser.

That is my best state *which my Saviour purchased and promised as best.* As he bought me not with silver and gold, so neither did he live and die to make me rich and great in the world. Who have more of these than they that have least of Christ? Is it heaven that cost so dear a price as his merits, sacrifice, and intercession? Is that the end of so wonderful a design of grace, and shall I now be unwilling to receive the gift?

That is best for me *for which God's Holy Spirit is preparing me.* He is not persuading me from day to day to love the world but to come off from it and to set my heart upon things above. And would I now undo all, or cross and frustrate all his operations? Has grace been so long preparing me for glory, and shall I be loth to take possession of it? If I am not willing, I am not yet sufficiently prepared.

If heaven be not better for me than earth, *God's Word and ordinances have been all in vain.* Surely that is my best which is the gift of the better covenant; which is secured to me by so many sealed promises; to which I am directed by so many sacred precepts, doctrines, and examples; and for which I have been called to hear and read, meditate, watch, and pray. Was it fleshly interest, or a longer life of worldly prosperity, which the gospel covenant secured to me; which the sacraments and Spirit sealed to me; which my books were written for; and for which I prayed, and served God? Or was it not for his grace on earth, and glory in heaven? And is it not better for me to have the end of these means than lose them and my hopes? Why have I used them, if I would not attain their end? That is my best state to which all God's fatherly providences tend. All his sweeter mercies and sharper corrections are to make me partaker of his holiness and lead me to glory in the way in which my Saviour and all his saints have gone before me.

'All things work together for the best' to me, by preparing me for that which is best indeed. Both calms and storms are to bring me to this harbour; if I take them but for themselves and for this present life, I mistake them, unthankfully vilify them, and lose their end, life, and sweetness. Every word and work of God, every day's mercies and changes, look at heaven and intend eternity. God leads me no other way; if I follow him not, I forsake my hope in forsaking him. If I follow him, shall I be unwilling to be at home, and arrive at the end of all this way?

Certainly that is best for me *which God requires me principally to value, love, and seek*. If my business in the world be only for the things of the world, how vain a creature is man, and how little is the difference between waking and sleeping, life and death! And is it my duty to *seek* heaven with all the fervour of my soul and diligence of my life, and is it not best to *find* it? That must needs be best for me, for the sake of which all other things must be forsaken. It is folly to forsake the better for the worse; but Scripture, reason, and conscience tell me that all this world should be forsaken for the least hope of heaven, when it comes in competition. A possible everlasting glory should be preferred before a certainly perishing vanity.

I am sure this life will shortly be nothing to me, and therefore it is nothing now. And must I forsake all for my everlasting hopes, and yet be unwilling to enter on the full possession? That is likely to be our best, which is our most mature state. Nature is ever tending towards perfection. Every fruit is best when it is ripe. And does God cause saints to grow to greater ripeness only to be useless? It is not credible. 'Our souls return to God that gave them'; and though he needs them not, he puts them to such heavenly uses as their maturity fits them for. Since love has ripened me for itself, shall I not willingly drop into its hand?

That is likely to be best which has been most esteemed and desired by the wisest and holiest in all ages, and which all men at death allow to be best. No men are usually worse than those who have no belief or hope of a life to come. And none are so holy, just and sober, so charitable to others, and so useful to mankind, as those who firmly believe in and hope for a state of immortality. And shall I fear such a state?

And is not that my best state, which most displeases my greatest enemies? I need not say how much Satan does to keep me and other men from heaven, and in order to that how he tempts us with worldly honour, pleasure, and wealth. Satan would not have me get to heaven, and shall I also be unwilling? All these things tell me, that it is best to be with Christ.

2. *As the end of all my preparation, it must be far better for me to be with Christ.* Is not dwelling with God in glory far better than in this sinful world? He that is our beginning is our end. For our end, all means are used. And the end attained is the rest of souls. How often has

my soul groaned under a sense of distance, darkness, and alienation from God! How often has it looked up, and panted after him and said, 'As the hart panteth after the water brooks, so panteth my soul after thee, O God: my soul thirsteth for God, for the living God; when shall I come and appear before God?' 'Whom have I in heaven but thee? and there is none upon earth that I desire besides thee . . . It is good for me to draw near to God.'

Woe to me, if I dissembled! If not, why should my soul draw back? Is it because death stands in the way? Do not my fellow-creatures die for my daily food? And is not my passage secured by the love of my Father, and the resurrection and intercession of my Lord? Can I see the light of heavenly glory in this darksome shell and womb of flesh?

All creatures are more or less excellent and glorious as God communicates most of himself to them. They are said to be nearest to him that have the noblest natures. Therefore to be as near as my nature was intended to approach is but to attain the end and perfection of my nature. As I am now under the government of his officers on earth, so I expect to be in heaven. If the law was given by angels, and the angel of God was in the burning bush, and the angel conducted the people through the wilderness, and yet all these things are ascribed to God; much more near and glorious will the divine government be in heaven. Here I am made, ruled, and sanctified for the good of many, as above my own. I am sure I must be finally for my glorified Redeemer; and that he who is the first will be the ultimate cause. In this respect I shall be as near to him, as is due to the rank and order of my nature. It is the honour of a servant to have an honourable master, and to be appointed to the most honourable work. My advancement will be ultimately for God, and in such services as are suitable to my spiritual and heavenly state.

Activity will be my perfection and my rest. Though now I know not fully what service I must do, I know it will be good, and suitable to the blessed state I shall be in. It is not all the use and work of my soul now to care for my body. Nor will it be hereafter. Though I shall not always have a body, I shall always have a God and a Saviour, and a world of fellow-creatures; and when I shine not in this lantern, nor see as in a glass, I shall yet see face to face. To fulfil God's will here would be the fulfilling of my own. I am sure my soul shall live, and that it shall live to God, and that I shall fulfil his blessed will; and so far as I am pleased in doing it, it will be my felicity.

The soul's regular love to the body illustrates the love of Christ to his church, and to every member. Herein my Saviour excels me in powerful, faithful love. He will save me better from pain and death than I can save my body, and will more inseparably hold me to himself. If it pleases my soul to dwell in such a house of clay, how much more will it please my glorified Lord to dwell with his glorified body, the church triumphant, and to bless each member of it! It would be a kind of death to Christ, to be separated from his body. And will he take incomparably greater pleasure in me for ever, than my soul does in my body? O then let me long to be with him!

Though I am naturally loth to be absent from the body, let me not be willingly absent from the Lord! And though I would not be unclothed, had not sin made it necessary, let me 'groan to be clothed upon with my heavenly habitation', to become the delight of my Redeemer, and to be perfectly loved by Love itself! The love and delight of my glorified Head must be my felicity. I shall be loved as a living spirit, and not as a thing dead and insensible. If I must rejoice here with them that rejoice, shall I not rejoice to have my Lord rejoice in me, and in all his glorified ones?

Union will make his pleasure to be much my own. It will fitly be said by him, 'Enter thou into the joy of thy Lord.' The heavenly society also will joyfully welcome a holy soul. If now 'there is joy in the presence of the angels of God, over one sinner that repenteth', what will there be over a perfect glorified soul? If 'our angels' there 'behold our Father's face', how glad will they be of our company! And will not love and union make their joy my own? Surely that will be my best condition which angels and blessed spirits will be best pleased with; and in that which they most rejoice, I shall most rejoice myself.

3. i. It is far better for me to be with Christ, as thereby *my knowledge will be perfected*. A soul that is with Christ is more likely to know Christ, and the Father in him, than a soul that is present with the body, and absent

from the Lord. What less can the promise of being with him signify? How much more excellent will intuitive or immediate knowledge be than our present artificial knowledge! There will be no expensive labour in getting it. It will have no mixture of dark and bewildering uncertainty and ambiguity when it is acquired. It will be perfectly free from those contentions which so much rob the ingenious of their time, destroy their love, hinder their minds from ascending to God and heavenly things, and fill the church with sects and parties. Nor will it leave any of that dissatisfaction, so common among the learned, while they have only the shadow of knowledge, licking but the outside of the glass, and leaving the wine within untasted.

What an excellency will there be in each of the objects of this immediate knowledge! As for instance: *I shall know God better*. If an angel from heaven came down on earth to tell us all of God that we would know, who would not turn his back on libraries and universities, to go and discourse with such a messenger? For one hour's talk with him, what travel should I think too far, what cost too great? But here we must only have such intimations as will exercise faith, excite desire, and try us under the temptations of the world and the flesh. The light of glory is to reward the victory obtained by the conduct of the light of grace. God in great mercy even here begins the reward. They that 'follow on to know the Lord' usually find such increase of light, not consisting in vain notions, but in the quickening and comforting knowledge of God, as greatly encourages them, and draws them still on to seek more. If the pleasure the mind has in common knowledge makes men spend successive years in traversing sea and land, or in turning over multitudes of tedious volumes, who then upon earth can possibly conceive how great a pleasure it will be for a glorified soul to see the Lord? All the pleasure I shall have in heaven in knowing any of the works of God, will be in my beholding God himself, his being, wisdom, love, and goodness, in those works; for he is the life and glory of them all. 'Blessed are the pure in heart, for they shall see God.'

And doubtless it will be no small part of my delight *to know the universe better*. It is exceedingly pleasant to know the least particle of the works of God. With what diligence and delight have men endeavoured to anatomize a body, yea, a small part of a carcase; or to know and describe worms and insects, plants and minerals! But no man ever yet perfectly knew the nature and uses of the least of them. If, indeed, we clearly saw the nature and connection of every creature in sea or land, what a delightful spectacle would this spot of the creation be! How much more to see the whole creation! And I shall have as much of this as I shall be capable of; the wonders of God's works shall raise my soul in admiring, joyful praise for ever.

We have desires after such knowledge, in our present dark and infant state, for 'the works of the LORD are great, sought out of all them that have pleasure therein.' As these desires are of God; as he hath made his works to be known for his glory; and as it is little that is known of them by mortals; therefore they are known by them in heaven, who are fitted to improve that knowledge to his praise. If Christ, the wisdom of God, will teach me the true philosophy, how to love God and please him in all things here, I shall quickly in heaven be a perfect philosopher. Satan tempted Christ by 'showing him all the kingdoms of the world, and the glory of them,' promising to 'give him all, if he would worship him'; but God will show me more than Satan could show; and give me more of that which is best than Satan could give.

Nor will it be the least of my felicity in heaven that *I shall better know Jesus Christ, and all the mystery of our redemption by him.* O beautifying knowledge! To know him, 'in whom are hid all the treasures of wisdom and knowledge'! To know the mystery of his eternal Godhead, of his created nature, and of the union of both, and to see God's wonderful design, and gracious work in him, laid open to our clearest view! Then all the dark texts concerning his Person, offices, and works will be fully understood. All those strange and difficult things which were the great exercise and honour of faith will then be plain. Difficulties will no more be Satan's advantage, to tempt us to unbelief or doubting. The sight of the glory of my Lord will be my glory. If now, 'though we see not Christ, yet believing, we love him, and rejoice in him with joy unspeakable and full of glory', what love and joy will the everlasting sight of our blessed Head excite there in the souls of all the glorified!

[69]

I shall better (O how much better!) know *the heavenly Jerusalem*, the triumphant church, the blessed angels and glorified saints. What a sight, what a joyful sight, will death show me, by drawing aside the veil; or rather the Lord of life, by turning death to my advantage! As I now know the several rooms in my house, so shall I then know the 'many mansions' which, Christ says, are 'in his Father's house'. If Nehemiah and the pious Jews rejoiced so much at seeing the walls of Jerusalem repaired, and others at the rebuilding the temple, O what a joyful sight shall I have of the heavenly Jerusalem!

I know that *angels* now love us, minister unto us, rejoice in our good, and are themselves far more holy and excellent creatures than we are; it is therefore my comfort to think that I shall better know them, and live in near and perpetual acquaintance and communion with them, and bear my part in the same choir in which they preside.

And when I think how sweet one wise and holy companion has been to me here on earth, and how lovely his graces have appeared, O what a sight it will be when we shall see the millions of the *'spirits of just men made perfect'* shining with Christ in perfect wisdom and holiness! If this world was full of wise, just, and holy persons, how lovely would it be! If one kingdom consisted of such, it would make us loth to die and leave such a country, were it not that the more the beauty of goodness appears the more the perfection of it is desired. It is pleasant to me to pray in hope that earth may be made more like heaven, which is now become so like hell; but when I shall see the society perfected in number, holiness, and glory, employed in the high and joyful praises of Jehovah, the glory of God and the Lamb shining on them, and God rejoicing over them as his delight, and myself partaking of the same, that will be the truly blessed day. And why does my soul, imprisoned in flesh, no more desire it?

I shall better understand *all the Word of God.* Though I shall not have that use for it as I now have in this life of faith, yet I shall see more of God's wisdom and goodness, love and mercy, and justice, appearing in it, than ever man on earth could do. As the creatures, so the Scriptures are perfectly known only by perfect spirits. I shall then know how to solve all doubts, reconcile all seeming contradictions, and expound the hardest prophecies. That light will show me the admirable method of those sacred words where dark minds now suspect confusion. How joyfully shall I then praise my God and Saviour for giving his church so clear a light to guide them through this darksome wilderness, and so sure a promise, to support them till they come to life eternal! How joyfully shall I bless him who, by that immortal seed, regenerated me to the hopes of glory and ruled me by so holy and just a law!

In that world of light I shall better understand *God's works of providence.* The wisdom and goodness of them is little understood in small parcels. It is the union and harmony of all the parts which displays the beauty of them. And no one can see the whole together but God, and they that see it in the light of his celestial glory. Then I shall clearly know why God prospered the wicked, and so much afflicted the righteous; why he set up the ungodly, and put the humble under their feet; why he permitted so much ignorance, pride, lust, oppression, persecution, falsehood, and other sins, in the world; why the faithful are so few; and why so many kingdoms of the world are left in heathenism, Mohammedanism, and infidelity. I shall know why I suffered what I did, and how many great deliverances I had, and how they were accomplished. All our misinterpretations of God's works and permissions will then be rectified, and all our controversies about them be at an end.

Among all these works, I shall especially know more of the nature and excellency of God's mercies. The lively sense of love and mercy makes lively Christians abound in love to God and in mercy to others; but the enemy of God and man labours to obscure and diminish our views of divine love and mercy. Ingratitude is great misery, as gratitude is true pleasure. We now receive thousands of mercies which we undervalue. But when I come to the state and work of perfect gratitude, I shall perfectly know all the mercies ever received by myself, by my neighbours and friends, by the church and the world. Mercies remembered must be the matter of our everlasting thanks, and we cannot be perfectly thankful for them, without a perfect knowledge of them.

The worth of Christ, and all his grace of the gospel, and of all divine ordinances and church privileges, of our books, and our friends, our health, and all the conveniences of our lives, will be better understood in heaven than the most holy and thankful Christian ever understood them here. Then I shall be much better acquainted with myself. I shall know the nature of souls, and the way of their operations, and how the Spirit of God works upon them, and how that Spirit is sent from Christ to work upon them. I shall know what measure of grace I myself had, and how far I was mistaken concerning it. I shall know more of the number and greatness of my sins, and of my obligation to pardoning and healing grace. Yea, I shall know more of my body, as the habitation of my soul, and how far it helped or hindered me, and what were all its diseases, and how wonderfully God supported, preserved, and often delivered me. I shall also far better know my fellow-creatures. The good and bad, the sincere and hypocrites, will there be discerned. Actions, that were here thought honourable, will then be found to be odious and unjust; and wickedness will no more be flattered or extenuated. Many a good and holy work which was reproached as criminal will there be justified, honoured and rewarded. Once more, I shall better know from what enemies, sins and dangers I was here delivered; what stratagems of Satan and his instruments God defeated; how many snares I escaped; and how great my deliverance by Christ from the wrath to come is.

All this knowledge will thus be advanced to my glorified soul, beyond my present conceptions; and is it not therefore far better to be with Christ?

3. ii. It is far better for me to be with Christ, *for the sake of having my will perfected.* The will is to the soul what the heart is to the body. My greatest evil is there, and there will be my greatest good. Satan did most against it, and God will do most for it. When I am with Christ, my will no more will be tied to a body, which is now the grand snare and enemy of my soul, by drawing my love and care, my fears and sorrows, to itself and turning them from my highest interest. There my will shall not be tempted by a world of inferior good; nor shall meat and sleep, possessions and friends, be my snares and dangers; nor shall the mercies of God be the tempter's instruments; nor shall I have the flatteries or frowns of tyrants; nor will bad company infect or divert me; nor the errors of good men seduce me; nor the reputation of the wise and learned draw me to imitate them in any sin. There will be none of Satan's solicitations to pervert my will.

My will shall there be better than here as it shall have *nothing in it displeasing to God*, no sinful inclination, no striving against God's Spirit, no grudging at any word or work of God, nor any principle of enmity or rebellion left. There it shall have no inclination to injure my neighbour, or to do any thing against the common good. And there it shall have nothing in it opposite to itself; no more 'law of my members warring against the law of my mind'; no more contrariety between sense and reason; but all will be unity and peace within.

There Christ will have perfectly sanctified my will and made it conformable to his own and to his Father's will.

This is at least his meaning when he prays that all his disciples may be one, 'as thou, Father, art in me, and I in thee, that they also may be one in us, that they may be one, even as we are one.' I shall love and will the same that God loves and wills. And how can the will of man have greater honour? Assimilation to an earthly king is honourable; much more to angels; but most of all to be like God. Indeed, here the divine image in us is, in its degrees, a conformity to the will of God. But, alas, how many thousand wishes and desires have we had which are against the will of God! We shall have the full impression of God's will in heaven, as face answers to face in a glass, or the wax to the seal, or the finger of the clock to the motion within, or as the echo to the voice. I shall desire, and never be disappointed. I shall have as much love and joy as I wish.

Before I desire anything, I shall know whether it be God's will or not, and therefore shall never wish anything that shall not be accomplished. Yea, my will shall be my enjoyment; for it shall not be the desire of what I want, but a complacency in what I possess. I shall want nothing. I shall thirst no more. Rightly is the will itself called love. My will shall be full of perfect joy, when enjoying love and pleasure will be my will. Thus shall I have in myself a spring of living waters.

My will shall be confirmed and fixed in this conformity to the will of God. Now, both understanding and will are so lamentably mutable that, further than God promises to uphold us, we know not one day what we shall think, judge or will the next. But when love becomes our fixed nature, we shall be no more weary of loving than the sun of shining. God himself will be the full and everlasting object of my love. Perfect joyful complacency in God, is the heaven which I desire and hope for. In God there is all that love can desire for its full everlasting feast. The nature of man's will is to love good as good. God who is infinitely good in himself will be that most suitable good to me. He has all in himself that I need or can desire.

There is nothing for love to cleave to either above him, beyond him, or outside him. He is willing to be beloved by me. He disdains not my love. He might have refused such affections as have so often embraced vanity and filth. But he commands my love, and makes it my greatest duty.

He invites and entreats me, as if he were a gainer by my happiness. He seeks me to seek him, and is both the first and most earnest suitor. He that so valued my cold imperfect love to him on earth will not reject my perfect love in heaven. And he is near to me, not a distant God out of my reach, nor unsuitable to my love.

Blind unbelievers may dream that he is far off; but even now he is as nigh to us as we are to ourselves. When he would sanctify us to love him, he brings us nigh to himself in Christ. Here we see him in his works and Word; and there we shall see him in all the perfect glory of his works, and shall delightfully love that glorious perfection of the universe, even the image of God in all the world.

I shall especially love the holy society, the triumphant universal church, consisting of Christ, angels, and saints.

God himself loves them more than his inferior works, and my love, according to its measure, will imitate his.

Think here, O my soul, how sweet thy condition will be, to love the Lord Jesus, thy glorified Head, with perfect love, when the glory of God, which shines in him, will feast thy love with full and everlasting pleasure! The highest created perfection of power, wisdom, and goodness, refulgent in him, will not permit thy love to cease, or abate its fervour. When thou shalt see in the glorified church, the precious fruits of Christ's redeeming grace and love; and when thou shalt see thyself possessed of perfect happiness, by his love to thee; and shalt remember what he did for thee, and in thee, here on earth; how he 'called thee with a holy calling'; how he 'washed thee in his blood from all thy sins'; how he kindled in thee desires after glory; how he renewed thy nature; how he instructed, guided, and preserved thee from sins, enemies, and sufferings; all this will constrain thee everlastingly to love him.

Think also, O my soul, how delightful it will be to love those angels, who most fervently love the Lord! They will be lovely to thee, as they have loved thee; and more, as they have been lovers of the church and of mankind; but far more as they are so many refulgent stars, which continually move, and shine, and burn, in perfect love to their Creator. O blessed difference between that amiable society, and this dark, distracted, wicked world! There I shall see or hear no evil, no mixture of folly or pollution; no false doctrine; no bad example; no favouring of wickedness nor accusing goodness; no hurtful violence; but holy, powerful, active love will be all, and do all, as their very nature, life, and work. And is not a day with them better than a thousand here?

And with holy angels, I shall also love holy souls, that are made like them, and joined with them in the same society. All their infirmities are there put off, and they also are spirits made up of holy life and light and love. When I think with what fervent love to God, to Jesus Christ, and to one another they will be perfectly united there, grieve and blush, O my soul, that they should be here so disaffected and divided, and hardly agree to call each other the servants of God, or to worship God in the same assemblies! The imperfect image of God upon them is amiable, but through their remaining pride, error, and uncharitableness it is hard to live with some of them in peace. O how delightful will that communion of saints be where perfect love shall make them one! Forget not, my soul, how sweet God has made the course of my pilgrimage, by the fragrance and usefulness of his servants' graces! How sweet have my bosom friends been! How sweet the neighbourhood of the godly! How sweet their holy assemblies, their writings, conference, and prayers! What then will it be to live in perfect love with perfect saints in heaven for ever, and with them perfectly to love the God of love!

As the act and object of love will constitute my future felicity, I shall not be the fountain of my own delights, but my receiving from the love of God and his creatures shall be sweeter to me than my own activity. All love is communicative, but none compared with God's. Whatever good is done in the world, it is done by love. Therefore parents care and provide for children. Therefore my house and table are not neglected, nor my books and learning forgot, nor my friends despised, nor my life itself thrown away. If a man love not his country, posterity, and the common good, he will be as a drone in the hive. And if created love be so necessary, so active and communicative, much more will the infinite love of the Creator. His love is now the life of nature in the living, the life of holiness in the saints, and the life of glory in them that are glorified.

In this love I and all the saints shall dwell for evermore. And if I dwell in love, and love in me, surely I shall 'ever drink of the rivers of pleasure'. Had I a great, wise and good friend that did for me the hundredth part of what God does, how dearly should I love him! Think, then, think believingly, seriously, constantly, O my soul, what a life thou shalt live for ever in the presence and bosom of infinite eternal Love! He now shineth on me by the sun, and on my soul by the Sun of righteousness, but it is as through the crevices of my darksome habitation; but then he will shine on me and in me openly, and with the fullest streams and beams of love. God is the same God in heaven as on earth, but I shall not be the same man. Here the windows of my soul are not open to his light; sin has raised clouds, and consequently storms, against my comforts. The entrances to my soul by the straits of flesh and sense are narrow, and they are made narrower by sin than they were by nature. Alas, how often would love have spoken comfortably to me, and I was not at home to be spoken with, but abroad among a world of vanities; or was not at leisure, or was asleep, and not willing to be awaked! How often would love have come in, and dwelt with me, and I have unkindly shut him out! How often would he have freely entertained me in secret, but I had some trifling company or business which I was loth to leave! When his table has been spread for me and Christ, grace and glory offered to me, how has my appetite been gone or dull! He would have been all to me, if I would have been all for him.

But in heaven I shall have none of these obstructions. All old unkindnesses and ingratitudes will be forgiven. I shall then be wholly separated from the vanity which here deceived me. I shall joyfully behold the open face and attend the charming voice of glorifying love and de-lightfully relish his celestial provisions. No disease will corrupt my appetite. No sluggishness will renew my guilty neglects. The love of the Father, the grace of the Son and the communion of the Holy Spirit will triumph over all my folly, deadness and disaffection; and my God-displeas-ing and self-undoing averseness and enmity will be gone for ever. Study this heavenly work of love, O my soul! These are not dead or barren studies. It is only love that can relish love, and understand it. Here the will has its taste. What can poor carnal worldlings know of glorious love, who study it without love? What sounding brass or tinkling cymbals are they that preach of God and Christ and heavenly glory without love! But gazing on the face of love in Christ, tasting its gifts, contemplating its glorious reign is the way to kindle the sacred fire in thee. The burning glass must be turned directly to the sun for it to set anything on fire. A holy love, like that in heaven, must be studiously fetched from heaven and be kindled by the foresight of what is there and what we shall be there for ever. Faith must ascend and look within the veil. Thou, my soul, must not live a stranger to thy home and hopes, to thy God and Saviour. The fire that must warm thee is in heaven, and thou must come near it and open thyself to its influence if thou wilt feel its powerful efficacy. It is night and winter with carnal minds when it is day and summer with those that set their faces heavenward.

But in heaven God will make use of second causes, even in communicating his love and glory. There the Lord Jesus Christ will not only be the object of our delightful love but his love to us will be as the vital heat and motion of the heart to all the members, the root of our life and joy. Did his tears for a dead Lazarus make men say, 'Behold how he loved him!' What then will the reviving beams of heavenly life make us say of that love which fills us with the pleasures of his presence, and turns our souls into joy itself? Believe, O my soul, thy Saviour's love, that thou mayest have a foretaste of it, and be fit for complete enjoyment. Let thy believing be so much of thy daily work that thou mayest say, 'He dwells in thy heart by faith' and 'lives in thee'. Look upon the sun and think with thyself how its motion, light and heat are communicated to millions of creatures all over the earth, and in the seas. What if all these beams of light and heat were proportionable beams of perfect knowledge, love and joy? If all the creatures under the sun received from it as much wisdom, love and joy as they have of light, heat and motion, what a blessed world would it be, even a heaven upon earth! Thus will the Sun of glory send forth life, light and joyful love on all the heavenly inhabitants.

Therefore now begin to live upon the influence of his grace, that thou mayest have his name and mark. He has not bid me seek his grace in vain. He more than bids me seek and ask. He teaches me to pray. He makes my prayers, and writes them on my heart. He gives me desires, and he loves to have me importunate with him, and is displeased with me that I will ask and have no more. How then comes my soul to be yet so fond of this wretched flesh and world, and so backward to go home and dwell with Christ? Alas! a taste of heaven on earth is too precious to be cast away upon such as have long grieved and quenched the Spirit, and are not, by diligent and patient seeking, prepared to receive it! My conscience remembers the follies of my youth, and many a later odious sin, and tells me that if heaven were quite hid from my sight, and I should never have a glimpse of the face of glorious eternal Love, it would be just. I look upward from day to day and, the better to know my God and my home, I cry to him daily, My God, my hopes are better than all the possessions of this world! Far better than all the pleasures of sin! Thy gracious looks have often revived me, and thy mercies have been unmeasurable to my soul and body. But O! how far am I short of what, even forty years ago, I hoped sooner to have attained! Where is 'the peace that passeth all understanding' which should keep my heart and mind 'through Christ Jesus'? Where is the seeing, longing, and rejoicing faith? Where is that pleasant familiarity with Christ and heaven, that would make a thought of them sweeter than the thoughts of friends, health, or all the prosperity and pleasure of this world? Do those that 'dwell in God, and God in them', and have their 'hearts and conversations in heaven', attain no more clear and satisfactory perceptions of that blessed state, than I have yet attained? Is there no livelier sense of future joys? No sweeter foretaste? No fuller silencing of doubts and fears? Alas! how many of thy servants are less afraid to go to a prison than to their God! And had rather be banished to a land of strangers, than sent to heaven!

Must I, that am called thy child and an heir of heaven and a co-heir with Christ, have no more acquaintance with my glorified Lord, and no more love to thee, who art my portion, before I go hence? Shall I have no more of the heavenly life, and light, and love? Alas! I have scarcely enough in my meditations, or prayers, or sermons, to denominate them heavenly! And must I go hence, so like a stranger to my home? Wilt thou take strangers into heaven, and know them there as thine who know thee no better here? O my God, vouchsafe a sinner yet more of the Spirit of thy Son, who came to earth to call up earthly minds to God, and to open heaven to all believers! What do I beg so frequently, so earnestly, for the sake of my Redeemer, as the Spirit of life and consolation, to show me the reconciled face of God and unite all my affections to my glorified Head, and draw up this dark, drowsy soul to love and long to be with thee?

Alas! though these are my daily groans, how little do I ascend! I dare not blame the God of love, nor my blessed Saviour, nor the Sanctifier and Comforter of souls. Undoubtedly the cause is my sinful resistance of the Spirit, my unthankful neglects of grace and glory. But mercy can forgive; grace can overcome; and may I not hope for such a victory before I die? Lord, I will lie at thy doors, and pour out my complaints before thee! Thou hast told us how kindly the dogs licked the sores of a Lazarus that lay at a rich man's gate; thou has commended the good Samaritan for taking care of a wounded man; thou sayest, 'Blessed are the merciful'; thou commandest us, 'Be merciful, as your heavenly Father is merciful'; and shall I wait at thy doors in vain? Give me the wedding garment, without which I shall but dishonour thy feast! Thou hast commanded me to rejoice, and how fain would I in this obey thee! O that I had more faithfully obeyed thee in ruling my senses, my thoughts, my tongue, and in the diligent improvement of all my talents! Then I might more easily have rejoiced.

Lord, help my love and joy! How can I rejoice in death and darkness? I hoped I was long since 'translated from the kingdom of darkness', and delivered from the power of the prince of darkness, and brought into that light, which is the entrance of the inheritance of saints; and yet, alas! darkness is still my misery! There is light round about me, in thy Word and works, but darkness is within me. And if my eye be dark, the sun will be no sun to me. What is my unbelief, but the darkness of my soul? Lord Jesus, scatter all these mists! O thou Sun of righteousness, make thy way into this benighted mind! O send thy Advocate to silence every temptation against thy truth and thee, to prosecute thy cause against thy enemies and mine, and to witness my sonship and salvation! I know, my Lord, heaven is not far from me, no, not a day, nor an hour's journey, to a separate soul. How quick is the communion of my eyes with the distant sun! And couldest thou not show me heaven in a moment?

Is not faith a seeing grace? If animated by thee, I can see the invisible God, the unseen world, the New Jerusalem, the innumerable company of angels and the spirits of just men made perfect. Without thee, it can do nothing, and is nothing. Forgive all my sins, and remove this film that sin hath gathered, and my enlightened soul will see thy glory! I know this veil of flesh must also be rent before I shall see thee with open face, and know my fellow-citizens above as I am known.

It is not heaven on earth I am asking, but that I may see it from mount Nebo, and have the pledge and the first-fruits; and that my faith and hope may kindle love and desire, and make me run my race with patience, and live and die in the joy which becomes an heir of heaven! But if my part on earth must not increase, let it make me the more weary of this dungeon, and more fervently wish for the day, when all my desires shall be satisfied, and my soul be filled with thy light and love!

And, in subordination to Christ, I shall also be a receiver in heaven from angels and saints. If angels are greatly useful to me here, much more will they be there, where I shall be more capable of receiving from them. It will be no more a diminution to the honour of Christ, to make use of my fellow-creatures to my joy there, than it was here. How gloriously will God shine in the glory of the blessed! How delightful will it be to see their perfection in wisdom, holiness, and love! They will love incomparably better than our dearest friends on earth can, who can only pity us in our pains, and go weeping with our corpses to the grave; but the friends above will joyfully convoy, or welcome, our souls to their triumphant society.

What a glorious state will it be when all the love of angels and saints in full perfection shall be so united as to make one love to one God, and to each other as made one in Christ! We little know how great a mercy it is here to be commanded to love our neighbours as ourselves; and much more to be effectually taught of God to love one another. Did we all live in such unfeigned love, earth would resemble heaven. Go, then, go willingly, O my soul! Love joins with light to draw up thy desires. Art thou a lover of wisdom, holiness and love, and wouldst thou not be united to the wise and holy who are made up of love? Art thou a hater of discord and divisions on earth, and wouldest thou not be where all the just are one? Is not thy body, while kept together by a uniting soul, in a better state than when it is to be crumbled into lifeless dust? And does not death creep on thee by a gradual dissolution? Away, then, from this incoherent state!

The further from the centre, the further from unity! It is now thy weakness and imperfection which makes thee so desirous that thy house, thy land, thy clothes, thy books, yea, thy knowledge and grace, should be thine and thine only. How much more excellent if thou couldest say that all these, like the light of the sun, are mine and everyone's as well as mine! In heaven, thy knowledge, thy glory, and felicity, shall be thine, and others as well as thine.

The knowledge, goodness and glory of all that perfect society, shall be thine, as far as thy capacity extends. Then hasten upwards, O my soul, with thy most fervent desires, and breathe after that state with thy strongest hopes, where thou shalt not be rich, and see thy neighbours poor; nor be poor while they are rich; nor be well, while they are sick; nor sick, while they are well! Communion, as it constitutes the very being of the city of God, will be part of every one's felicity, and none will have the less for the participation of the rest. This celestial communion of saints in one holy church, above what is here attainable, is now an article of our belief; but believing will soon end in seeing and enjoying.

3. iii. It is also far better for me to be with Christ *that I may have a perfect activity in doing good*. There are good works in heaven, and far more and better than on earth. There will be more life and power for action; more love to God and one another to excite to action; more likeness to God and Christ in doing good, as well as being good; more union with the beneficent Jesus to make us also beneficent; and more communion by each contributing to the welfare of the whole and sharing in their common returns to God. What the heavenly works are, we must perfectly know when we come thither. We shall join with the whole society, as Scripture particularly describes, in giving thanks and praise to God and our Redeemer.

All passions earnestly desire to be freely exercised, especially our holy affections of love, joy, and admiration of Almighty God. In expressing such affections, we naturally desire communion with many. Methinks, when we are singing the praises of God in great assemblies with joyful and fervent spirits, we have the liveliest foretaste of heaven upon earth, and could almost wish that our voices were loud enough to reach through all the world, and to heaven itself. Nor could I ever be offended with the sober and seasonable use of instrumental music to help to tune my soul in so holy a work, in which no true assistance is to be despised.

Nothing comforts me more in my greatest sufferings, nor seems more fit for me while I wait for death, than singing psalms of praise to God, nor is there any exercise in which I had rather end my life. Should I not then willingly go to the heavenly choir where God is praised with perfect love and joy and harmony? Had I more of a praising frame of soul, I should long more for that life of praise. I never find myself more willing to be there than when I most joyfully speak or sing the praises of God. Though 'the dead praise not God in the grave, nor does dust celebrate him', yet living souls in heaven do it joyfully, while their fleshly clothing turns to dust. Lord, tune my soul to thy praises now, that sweet experience may make me long to be where I shall do it better!

Wherever there is any excellent music, I see men naturally flock to it and hear it with delight. Surely had I once heard the heavenly choir, I should echo to their holy songs, and think it the truest blessedness to bear my part. My God, it is the inward melody of thy Spirit, and my own conscience, that must tune me for the heavenly melody. O speak thy love first to my heart, and then I shall joyfully speak it to others, and shall ardently seek after communion, better than that of sinful mortals! Though my sins make a sad discord in my present songs, I hope my sighs and tears for sin have had the honour of thine acceptance, who despisest not a contrite soul. But if thy Spirit will sing and speak within me, and help me against the jarring murmurs of my unbelieving heart and pained flesh, I shall then offer thee what is more suitable to thy love and grace.

I confess, Lord, that daily tears and sighs are not unsuitable to the eyes and voice of so great a sinner, now under the correcting rod. But 'he that offereth praise glorifies thee'; and is not this the 'spiritual sacrifice, acceptable through Christ', for which we are made priests to God? I refuse not, Lord, to lie in tears and groans when thou requirest it, nor do thou reject those tears and groans; but O give me better, that I may have better of thine own to offer thee, and so prepare me for the far better which I shall find with Christ!

Probably God makes glorified spirits the agents of his beneficence to inferior creatures. Where he bestows on any the noblest endowments, we see he makes most use of such for the benefit of others. Christ tells us we shall be like or equal to the angels, who are evidently the ministers of God for the good of his people in this world. The apostle says the saints shall judge the world, and angels; intimating, that devils and damned spirits shall be subjected to the saints.

But if there were no more for us to do in heaven but with perfect knowledge, love and joy to hold communion with God and all the heavenly society, it is enough to excite, in a considerate soul, the most fervent desires to be at home with God.

5

GOD MAKES US WILLING TO DEPART

I am convinced that it is far better to depart and to be with Christ than to be here. But this conviction alone will not excite such desires in my soul. They are opposed by a natural aversion to death which sin has greatly increased; by the remains of unbelief, which avails itself of our darkness in the flesh and our too-great familiarity with this visible world; and also by the want of our more lively foretastes of heaven.

What must be done to overcome this opposition? Is there no remedy? Yes, there is a divine teaching by which we must learn 'so to number our days that we may apply our hearts unto wisdom'. When we have read and heard, spoken and written the soundest truth and strongest arguments, we still know as if we knew not, and believe as if we believed not, unless God powerfully impresses the same things on our minds and awakens our souls to feel what we know. Since we fell from God, the communion between our senses and understanding, and also between our understanding and our will and affections, is violated; and we are divided in ourselves by this schism in our faculties.

All men may easily know that there is an almighty, omniscient, omnipresent, eternal, and perfectly holy and good God, the Maker, Preserver, and Governor of all, who deserves our whole trust, love, and obedience; but how little of this knowledge is to be perceived in men's hearts or lives! All men know that the world is vanity, that man must die, that riches cannot then profit, that time is precious, and that we have but little time to prepare for eternity; but how little do men seem to have of the real knowledge of these plain truths! Indeed, when God comes in with his powerful, awakening light and love, then those things appear as different as if we were beginning to know them.

All my best reasons for our immortality, are but as the new-formed body of Adam before 'God breathed into him the breath of life'; and he only can make them living reasons. To the Father of lights I must therefore still look up, and for his light and love I must still wait. I must learn both as a student and a beggar. When I have thought and thought a thousand times, I must beg thy blessing, Lord, upon my thoughts. The eye of my understanding will be useless or vexatious to me, without thy illuminating beams. O shine the soul of thy servant into a clearer knowledge of thyself and kingdom, and love him into more divine and heavenly love, and he will then willingly come to thee!

Why should I, by the fears of death, strive against the common course of nature and against my only hopes of happiness? Is it not 'appointed unto men once to die'? Would I have God make sinful man immortal upon earth? When we are sinless, we shall be immortal. The love of life was given to teach me to preserve it with care, and use it well, and not to torment myself with the continual foresight of death. If it be the misery after death that is feared, O what have I to do, but to receive the free, reconciling grace, which is offered me from heaven, to save me from such misery; and to devote myself totally to him, who has promised, 'Him that cometh to me I will in no wise cast out'? Had I studied my duty, and remembered that I am not my own, and that my times are in God's hands, I had been quiet from these fruitless fears. Had my resignation and devotedness to God been more absolute, my trust in him would have been more easy. But, Lord, thou knowest, that I would fain be thine, and wholly thine, and that to thee I desire to live: therefore let me quietly die to thee, and wholly trust thee with my soul.

Why should I have any remaining doubt of the future state of pious separate spirits? My Saviour has entered into the holiest, and has assured me that there are many mansions in his Father's house, and that when we are 'absent from the body' we shall be 'present with the Lord'. Who can think that all holy souls that have gone hence from the beginning of the world have been deceived in their faith and hope? And that all those whose hope was only in this life have been in the right? Shall I not abhor every suggestion that contains such absurdities? Wonderful, that Satan can keep up so much unbelief in the world, while he must make men fools in order to make them unbelievers and ungodly!

That my soul has no more lively foretastes of heaven arises from *those many wilful sins by which I have quenched the Spirit, and from the soul's imprisonment in the flesh*. This, O this, is the misery and burden of my soul! Though I can say I love God's truth and graces, his work and servants, yet, that I have no more ardent and delightful love of heaven where his loveliness will be more fully opened to my soul is my sin, calamity, and shame. If I did not see that it is so with others of the servants of Christ as well as myself, I should doubt whether affections so disproportionate to my profession did not imply an unsound faith.

It is strange that one who expects quickly to see the glorious world and enter the holy, celestial society should not be more joyfully affected with such hopes! And that I should think so much of the pain and perishing of the flesh, though it be the common way to such an end! O hateful sin, that has so darkened and corrupted souls, as to indispose them for their only expected happiness! What did man do when he forsook the love and obedience of his God? How just, that this flesh should be our prison which we are for making our home! How mournful, that there is no more grace and holiness, knowledge of God and communion with him, in this world! That so few are saints, and those few so very imperfect! That while the sun shines on all the earth, the Sun of righteousness shines on so small a part of it!

He that made us capable of holy and heavenly affections gave us not that capacity in vain. Yet, alas, how little of God and glory enters into the hearts of men! When recovering light shines upon us, how unthankfully do we entertain it! We cannot have the conduct and comfort of it while we shut our eyes, and turn away. And though God give to the best not so much of it as they desire, it is an unspeakable mercy that in this darksome world we may but hear of a better world, and may seek it in hope. We must not grudge in our prison to be denied such a presence of our King, and such pleasures of the kingdom, as innocent and free subjects have. Hope of pardon, and of a speedy deliverance, are great mercies to malefactors. And if my want of the knowledge and love of God and of joyful communion with the heavenly society be my prison, and as the suburbs of hell, should it not make me long for the day of my redemption, and the glorious liberty of the sons of God? My sincere desires of deliverance, and of holiness and perfection, are my evidences that I shall obtain them.

As the will is the sinner, so the obstinate continuance of a will to sin is the cause of continued sin. So far as God makes us willing to be delivered from sin, so far we are delivered, and our imperfect deliverance is the way to more. If pains make me groan for ease, and sickness for health, why should not my remains of ignorance, unbelief and alienation from God excite my desire after the day of my salvation? As it is the nature of my sin to draw down my heart from God and glory; so it is the nature of my faith, hope, and love to raise my heart towards heavenly perfection; not to desire death, but that which is beyond it. And have I been so many years in the school of Christ, learning both how to live and die, praying for this grace, and exercising it against this sinful flesh; and after all, shall I find flesh more powerful to draw me downward than faith, hope, and love, to carry my desires up to God? O God, forbid! O thou, that freely gavest me thy grace, maintain it to the last against its enemies, and make it finally victorious!

It came from thee; it has been preserved by thee; it is on thy side and wholly for thee; without it, I had lived as a beast, and should die more miserably than a beast; it is thine image that thou lovest; it is a divine nature and a heavenly beam. What will a soul be without it, but a dungeon of darkness, and dead to holiness and heaven? Without it, who shall plead thy cause against the devil, world, and flesh? Without thy glory, earth is but earth; and without thy grace, earth would be a hell. O, rather deny me the light of the sun, than the light of thy countenance! Less miserable had I been without life or being than without thy grace. Without thine and my Saviour's help, I can do nothing. I could not pray or learn without thee; I never could conquer a temptation without thee; and can I die, or be prepared to die, without thee? I shall but say, as Thomas to Christ, I know not whither my soul is going, and how can I know the way? My Lord, having loved his own which were in the world, he loved them unto the end. He even commended and rewarded those that had continued with him in his temptations. Thou lovest fidelity and perseverance in thy servants; and wilt thou forsake a sinner in his extremity, who consents to thy covenant, and would not forsake thee?

My God, I have often sinned against thee, but thou knowest I would fain be thine. I can say with Paul, Thou art the God 'whose I am, and whom I serve'; and O that I could serve thee better! To serve thee is but to receive thy grace and use it for my own and others' good, and thereby please and glorify thee. I have nothing to do in this world but to seek and serve thee. I have nothing to do with my tongue, but to speak to thee and for thee; and with my pen but to publish thy glory and thy will. What have I to do with all my reputation and influence over others but to increase thy church and propagate thy holy truth and service? What have I to do with my remaining time, even these last and languishing hours, but to look up unto thee and wait for thy grace and thy salvation? O pardon all my carnal thoughts, all my unthankful treatment of thy grace and love, and all my wilful sins against thy truth and thee! Under the terrors of the law thou didst even proclaim thyself, 'The LORD, the LORD God, merciful and gracious, long-suffering, and abundant in goodness and truth; keeping mercy for thousands, forgiving iniquity, transgression, and sin.' And is not 'the grace of our Lord Jesus Christ' revealed in the gospel, for our more abundant faith and consolation?

My God, I know I can never be sufficiently confident of thy all-sufficient power, wisdom, and goodness. When I have said, 'Will the LORD cast off for ever? And will he be favourable no more? Is his mercy clean gone for ever? Doth his promise fail for evermore? Hath God forgotten to be gracious? Hath he in anger shut up his tender mercies?', conscience has replied, 'This is mine infirmity, I never wanted comfort for want of mercy in thee, but for want of faith and holiness in myself. And hast thou not mercy also to give me that faith and holiness? My God, all is of thee, and through thee, and to thee, and when I have the felicity, the glory of all for ever will be thine. None that trust in thy nature and promise shall be ashamed. If I can live and die trusting in thee, surely I shall not be confounded.'

Why then should it seem a difficult question, how my soul may willingly leave this world and go to Christ in peace? The same grace which regenerated me must bring me to my desired end. Believe and trust thy Father, thy Saviour, and thy Comforter. Hope for the joyful entertainments of the promised blessedness. And long by love for nearer divine union and communion. Thus, O my soul, mayest thou depart in peace.

Believe and trust the promise of God. How sure it is, and how suitable to his love, to the nature of our souls, and to the operations of every grace! Why, O my soul, art thou so vainly solicitous to have clear, distinct conceptions of the celestial world? When thou art possessed of a better state, thou shalt know it as a possessor ought to do; for such a knowledge as thou lookest after, is part of the possession. Thy Saviour and his glorified saints are possessors. His knowledge must now be thy chief satisfaction. Seek not vainly to usurp his prerogative. Wouldst thou be a God and Saviour to thyself? Consider how much of the Fall there is in this selfish desire to be as God, in knowing that which belongs not to thee to know. Thou knowest that there undoubtedly is a God of infinite perfection, and that he is 'a Rewarder of them that diligently seek him'. Labour more to know thy duty to this God, and absolutely trust him as to the particulars of thy reward.

Thou didst trust thy parents to provide thee food and raiment, and didst implicitly obey them. Thou hast trusted physicians to give thee medicines, without inquiring after every ingredient. If a pilot undertakes to carry thee to the Indies, thou canst trust his conduct without knowing either the ship or how to govern it or the way or the place to which thou art conveyed. And must not thy God and Saviour be trusted to bring thee safe to heaven, unless he will satisfy all thy inquiries? The command, to 'be careful for nothing', and to 'cast all thy care on God, who careth for thee', obligeth thee in all things that are God's part. To dispose of a departing soul is God's part. O how much evil is there in this distrusting, self-providing care! Be not cast down, O departing soul, nor by unbelief disquieted within me. Trust thou in God, for soon shall experience teach thee to praise him who is 'the health of my countenance, and my God'.

How clearly does *reason* command me to trust him, absolutely and implicitly to trust him, and to distrust myself? He is essential, infinite perfection, wisdom, power, and love. There is nothing to be trusted in any creature, but God working in it, or by it. I am altogether his own by right, by devotion, and by consent. He is the Giver of all good to every creature, as freely as the sun gives its light; and shall we not trust the sun to shine? He is my Father and has taken me into his family, and shall I not trust my heavenly Father? He has given me his Son, as the greatest pledge of his love, and 'shall he not with him also freely give me all things'?

His Son purposely came to reveal his Father's unspeakable love, and shall I not trust him who has proclaimed his love by such a messenger from heaven? He has given me the Spirit of his Son, even the Spirit of adoption, the witness, pledge, and earnest of heaven, the seal of God upon me, 'holiness to the Lord', and shall I not believe his love, and trust him? He has made me a member of his Son, and will he not take care of me, and is not Christ to be trusted with his members? I am his interest, and the interest of his Son, freely beloved and dearly bought, and may I not trust him with his treasure? He has made me the care of angels, who rejoiced at my repentance, and shall they lose their joy or ministration? He is in covenant with me, and has given me many 'great and precious promises', and can he be unfaithful? My Saviour is the forerunner, who has entered into the holiest, and is there interceding for me, having first conquered death to assure us of a future life, and ascended into heaven, to show us whither we must ascend, and having said to his brethren, 'I ascend to my Father and your Father, to my God and your God'; and shall I not follow him through death, and trust such a Guide and Captain of my salvation? He is there to 'prepare a place for me, and will receive me unto himself,' and may I not confidently expect it? He told a malefactor on the cross, 'Today shalt thou be with me in paradise', to show believing sinners what they may expect. His apostles and other saints have served him on earth with all these expectations. 'The spirits of just men made perfect' are now possessing what I hope for, and I am a follower of them who 'through faith and patience inherit' the promised felicity; and may I not trust him to save me, who has already saved millions? I must be at the divine disposal, whether I will or not; and however I vex my soul with fears and cares and sorrows, I shall never prevail against the will of God, which is the only rest of souls. Our own wills have undone us and are our disease, our prison, and our death, till they are brought over to the will of God; and shall I die distrustfully striving against his will, and preferring my own before it?

What abundant *experience* have I had of God's fidelity and love, and after all, shall I not trust him? His undeserved mercy gave me being, chose my parents, gave them affectionate desires for my real good, taught them to instruct me early in his Word, and educate me in his fear, made my habitation and companions suitable, endowed me with a teachable disposition, put excellent books into my hands, and placed me under wise and faithful school-masters and ministers.

His mercy fixed me in the best of lands, and in the best age that land had seen. His mercy early destroyed in me all great expectations from the world, taught me to bear the yoke from my youth, caused me rather to groan un-der my infirmities than struggle with the powerful lusts, and chastened me betimes but did not give me over unto death. Ever since I was at the age of nineteen, great mercy has trained me up in the school of affliction to keep my sluggish soul awake in the constant expectation of my change, to kill my proud and worldly thoughts, and to direct all my studies to things the most necessary.

How has a life of constant but gentle chastisement, urged me to 'make my calling and election sure', and to prepare my accounts, as one that must quickly give them up to God! The face of death and nearness of eternity convinced me what books to read, what studies to pros-ecute, what companions to choose; drove me early into the vineyard of the Lord; and taught me to preach as a dying man to dying men. It was divine love and mer-cy which made sacred truth so pleasant to me that my life, under all my infirmities, has been almost a constant recreation. How far beyond my expectation has a mer-ciful God encouraged me in his sacred work, choosing every place of my ministry and abode to this day, without my own seeking, and never sending me to labour in vain! How many are gone to heaven and how many are in the way through a divine blessing on the Word which in weakness I delivered! Many good Christians are glad of now and then an hour to meditate on God's Word and refresh themselves in his holy worship, but God has allowed and called me to make it the constant business of my life. In my library I have profitably and pleasantly dwelt among the shining lights with which the learned, wise and holy men of all ages have illuminated the world. How many comfortable hours have I had in the society of living saints, and in the love of faithful friends! How many joyful days in solemn, worshipping assemblies where the Spirit of Christ has been manifestly present, both with ministers and people! How unworthy was such a sinful worm as I who never had any academical helps, nor much from the mouth of any teacher, that books should become so great a blessing to me, and that God should use me above forty years in so comfortable a work as pleading and writing for love, peace and concord, and with so much success!

What mercy had I amidst the calamities of a civil war to live two years in safety at Coventry, a city of defence, and in the heart of the kingdom! When I afterwards saw the effects of human folly and fury and of God's displeasure in the ruin of towns and countries, and in fields covered with carcases of the slain, how mercifully was I preserved, and brought home in peace! And oh! How great was the mercy showed me in a peaceable, humble, unanimous people, so numerous, so exemplary, and who to this day maintain their integrity and concord when, for thirty-one years, I have been forced to remain at a distance from them! What a mercy when I might not speak by voice to any single congregation to be enabled to speak by writings to many and to have the plainest writings attended with success, and some of them sent to preach in foreign lands and languages! Though I have been sent to the common jail for my service and obedience to God, yet he has there kept me in peace and soon delivered me: and how often has he succoured me, when nature and art have failed!

How has he cured my consumptive coughs, stopped my flowing blood, eased my pained limbs, and upheld an emaciated skeleton! I have had fifty years added to my days, though I expected not to live one of them; and what strange deliverances have been wrought for me, upon the importunate requests of many hundreds of my praying friends! How have I been kept in ordinary health and safety, when the raging pestilence came near my hab-it–ation and consumed a hundred thousand citizens! And how was my dwelling preserved when I saw London, the glory of the land, in flames! These, and many more, are my experiences of that wonderful mercy which has meas-ured my pilgrimage, and filled up my days. Never did God break his promise with me. Never did he fail me, or forsake me. And shall I now distrust him at last?

To thee, O Lord, as to 'a faithful Creator', I commit my soul. I know that thou art 'the faithful God, which keep-eth covenant and mercy with them that love thee, and keep thy commandments'. Thou art faithful, who hast called me to the fellowship of thy Son Jesus Christ our Lord. Thy faithfulness has saved me from temptation and kept me from prevailing evil and will 'preserve my whole spirit and soul and body, unto the coming of Christ. It is in faithfulness thou hast afflicted me, and shall I not trust thee to save me?

It is thy faithful saying, that thy elect shall obtain the salvation which is in Christ Jesus, with eternal glory; for 'if we be dead with him, we shall also live with him; if we suffer, we shall also reign with him'. To thee, O my Saviour, I commit my soul; it is thine by redemption, thine by covenant; it is sealed by thy Spirit, and thou hast promised not to lose it. Thou wast 'made like unto thy brethren, that thou mightest be a merciful and faithful High Priest in things pertaining to God, to make reconciliation for our sins'. By thy blood we have 'boldness to enter into the holiest, by a new and living way consecrated for us'. Cause me to draw near with a true heart, in full assurance of faith. Thy name is faithful and true. True and faithful are all thy promises. Thou hast promised rest to weary souls that come to thee. I am weary of suffering, sin, and flesh; weary of my darkness, dullness, and distance.

Whither should I look for rest, but home to my heavenly Father and thee? I am but a bruised reed, but thou wilt not break me. I am but smoking flax, but thou wilt not quench what thy grace hath kindled. Thou in whose name the nations trust wilt 'bring forth judgment unto victory'. The Lord redeems the souls of his servants, and none of them that trust in him shall be desolate. I will wait on thy name, for it is good; I trust in the mercy of God for ever and ever. The Lord is good, a stronghold in the day of trouble, and he knoweth them that trust in him. Sinful fear brings a snare, but whoso putteth his trust in the Lord shall be safe. Blessed is the man that maketh the Lord his trust. Thou art my hope, O Lord God, thou art my trust from my youth. By thee have I been holden up from the womb, my praise shall be continually of thee. Cast me not off in the time of old age, forsake me not when my strength faileth.

O God! Thou hast taught me from my youth, and hitherto have I declared thy wondrous works. Now also, when I am old and grey-headed, O God, forsake me not. Mine eyes are unto thee, O God, the Lord! In thee is my trust, leave not my soul destitute. I had fainted, unless I had believed to see the goodness of the Lord in the land of the living, even where they that live shall die no more. The sun may cease to shine on man, and the earth to bear us; but God will never cease to be faithful to his promises. Blessed be the Lord, who has commanded me so safe and quieting a duty as to trust in him and cast all my cares upon him who has promised to care for me!

Hope also for the salvation of God. Hope is the ease, yea, the life of our hearts which would otherwise break and even die within us. Despair is no small part of hell. God cherishes hope as he is the lover of souls. Satan, our enemy, cherishes despair when his more usual way of presumption fails. Hope anticipates salvation, as fear does evil. It is the hypocrite's hope that perishes; and all who hope for durable happiness on earth must be deceived. But, 'Happy is he that hath the God of Jacob for his help, whose hope is in the LORD his God, which made heaven and earth, which keepeth truth for ever.' Woe to me if in this life only I had hope. But the righteous hath hope in his death. And hope maketh not ashamed. 'Blessed is the man that trusteth in the LORD, and whose hope the LORD is.'

Lay hold then, O my soul, upon the hope set before thee; it is thy sure and steadfast anchor without which thou wilt be as a shipwrecked vessel. Thy foundation is sure, even God himself. Our faith and hope are both in God. Christ, who dwells in our hearts by faith, is in us the hope of glory. By this hope, better than the law of Moses could bring, we draw nigh unto God. We hope for that we see not, and with patience wait for it.

We are saved by hope. It is an encouraging grace, it excites our diligence, and helps to full assurance unto the end. It is a desiring grace, and is an earnest to obtain the glory hoped for. It is a comforting grace, for the God of hope fills us 'with all joy and peace in believing, that we may abound in hope through the power of the Holy Ghost'.

Shake off despondency, O my soul, and 'rejoice in hope of the glory of God'. Believe in hope, though dying flesh would tell thee that it is against hope.

What blessed preparations are made for our hope! God has confirmed it by two immutable things, his promise and his oath. His abundant mercy hath 'begotten us again unto a lively hope, by the resurrection of Christ, to an inheritance incorruptible, and undefiled, and that fadeth not away, reserved in heaven for us'. Grace teacheth us, that 'denying ungodliness and worldly lusts, we should live soberly, righteously, and godly in this present world; looking for that blessed hope, and the glorious appearing of the great God and our Saviour'. We are renewed by the Holy Ghost, and justified by grace, that we should be made heirs according to the hope of eternal life. The eyes of our understanding are enlightened that we may know what is the hope of his calling, and what the riches of the glory of his inheritance in the saints. The hope which is laid up for us in heaven, hath through the gospel, brought life and immortality to light. Having hope toward God, we exercise ourselves to have always a conscience void of offence, and serve God day and night. For an helmet, we put on the hope of salvation.

Death is not to us as it is to others which 'have no hope'. Our Lord Jesus Christ and God, even our Father, hath loved us and hath given us everlasting consolation, and good hope through grace, to comfort our hearts, and stablish us in every good word and work. We must hold fast the rejoicing of the hope firm unto the end, and continue in the faith grounded and settled, and not be moved away from the hope of the gospel. And now, Lord, what wait I for? My hope is in thee.

Uphold me according to thy Word that I may live, and let me not be ashamed of my hope. Though our iniquities testify against us, yet, O Lord, the Hope of Israel, the Saviour therof in time of trouble, be not as a stranger; leave us not. We have been showed the praises of the Lord, and his wonderful works, that we might set our hope in God. 'Remember the word unto thy servant, upon which thou hast caused me to hope.' 'If thou, LORD, shouldest mark iniquities, O Lord, who shall stand? But there is forgiveness with thee, that thou mayest be feared. I wait for the Lord, my soul doth wait, and in his word do I hope. Let Israel hope in the LORD, for with the LORD there is mercy, and with him is plenteous redemption.' 'The LORD taketh pleasure in them that fear him, in those that hope in his mercy.' Though my flesh and heart faileth, God is the strength of my heart. 'The LORD is my portion, saith my soul, therefore will I hope in him.' 'The LORD is good unto them that wait for him, to the soul that seeketh him. It is good that a man should both hope, and quietly wait for the salvation of the LORD. It is good for a man that he bear the yoke in his youth . . . he putteth his mouth in the dust, if so be there may be hope.'

God need not flatter such worms as we are, nor promise us what he never means to perform. He has laid the rudiments of our hope in a nature capable of desiring, seeking and thinking of another life. He has called me by grace to actual desires and endeavours, and has vouchsafed some foretastes. I look for no heaven but the perfection of divine life, light, and love in endless glory, with Christ and his saints, and this he has already begun in me. And shall I not boldly hope, when I have capacity, the promise, and the earnest and foretaste? Is it not God himself that caused me to hope? Was not nature, promise, and grace from him? And can a soul miscarry and be deceived that departs hence in a hope of God's own producing and encouraging? Lord, I have lived in hope, I have prayed, laboured, suffered, and waited in hope, and by thy grace I will die in hope; and is not this according to thy word and will? And wilt thou cast away a soul that hopes in thee, by thine own command and operation?

Had wealth and honour and continuance on earth or the favour of man been my reward and hope, my hope and I had died together. Were this our best, how vain were man! But the Lord liveth, and my Redeemer is glorified and intercedes for me: and the same Spirit is in heaven who is in my heart, as the same sun is in the firmament and in my house. The promise is sure to all Christ's seed; for millions are now in heaven who once lived and died in hope. They were sinners once, as I now am; they had no other Saviour, Sanctifier, or promise than I now have. Confessing that they were strangers and pilgrims on the earth, they desired a better country, that is, a heavenly, where they now are. And shall I not follow them in hope, who have sped so well?

Then, O my soul, hope unto the end. Hope in the Lord, from henceforth and for ever. I will hope continually, and will yet praise him more and more. My mouth shall show forth his righteousness and salvation. The Lord is at my right hand, I shall not be moved. Therefore my heart is glad, and my glory rejoiceth, my flesh also shall rest in hope. God hath showed me the path of life; in his presence is fulness of joy, and at his right hand there are pleasures for evermore.

What then remains, but that, in faith and hope, I love my God, my Saviour, my Comforter, the glorious society, and my own perfection in glory, better than this burden of flesh, and this howling wilderness?

How odious is that darkness and unbelief, that unholiness and disaffection, that deadness and stupidity, which makes such love seem hard and unsuitable! Is it unsuitable or hard for the eye to see the light or the beauties of creation, or for a man to love his life, or health, his father, or his friend? What should be easier to a nature that has rational love than to love him who is Love itself? He that loveth all and gives to all a capacity to love should be loved by all; and he that hath especially loved me, should especially be loved by me.

Love desires to please God, and therefore to be in the most pleasing state and freed from all that is displeasing to him; which is not to be hoped for on earth. It desires all suitable nearness, acquaintance, union, and communion. It is weary of distance and alienation. It takes advantage of every notice of God to renew and exercise these desires. Every message and mercy from God is fuel for love and, while we are short of perfection, stirs up our desires after more of God. The soul is where it loves.

If our friends dwell in our hearts by love; and if fleshly pleasures, riches and honour dwell in the hearts of the voluptuous, covetous and proud, surely God and Christ, heaven and holiness, dwell in the heart which loves them fervently. And if heaven dwell in my heart, shall I not desire to dwell in heaven?

If divine love would more plentifully pour itself upon my heart, how easy would it be to leave this flesh and world! Death and the grave would be but a triumph for victorious love. It would be easier to die in peace and joy, than to go to rest at night after a fatiguing day, or eat when I am hungry. A little love has made me willingly study, preach, write and even suffer; and would not more love make me willingly go to God? Shall the imagination of house, gardens, walks, libraries, prospects, etc. allure the desires of deceived minds, and shall not the thoughts of heavenly mansions, converse, and joys more power-fully draw up my desires?

Can I love such a world as this, where tyranny sheds streams of blood, and lays cities and countries deso-late; where the wicked are exalted, the just and innocent reproached and oppressed, the gospel restrained, idola-try and infidelity too generally kept up; where Satan too often chooses pastors for the churches of Christ, even such as by ignorance, pride, and sensuality, become devouring wolves to those whom they should feed and comfort; where no two persons are in all things of a mind, and where appears but little hopes of a remedy? And shall I not think more delightfully of 'the inheritance of the saints in light' and of the cordial love and joyful praises of the church triumphant? Should I not love a lovely and loving world much better than a world where there is comparatively so little loveliness or love?

All that is of God is good and lovely. But here his glory shines not in felicitating splendour. I am taught to look upward when I pray, 'Our Father, which art in heaven.' God's works are amiable, even in hell; and yet though I would know them, I would not be there. And, alas! how much of the works of man is here mixed with the works of God! Here is God's wisdom, but man's folly; God's government, but man's tyranny; God's love and mercy, but man's wrath and cruelty; much of God's beautiful order and harmony, but much of man's deformity and confusion.

Here is much truth and justice, but how it is mixed! Here are wise, judicious teachers and companions, but comparatively how few! Here are worthy and religious families; but by the temptations of wealth, and worldly interest, how full even of 'the sins of Sodom, pride, fulness of bread, and abundance of idleness', if not also of unmercifulness to the poor! And how few pious families of the great that do not quickly degenerate from their progenitors by error or sensuality! Here are some that educate their children wisely in the fear of God, and accordingly have comfort in them; but how many are there that, having devoted them to God in baptism, train them up to the service of the world, the flesh, and the devil!

How many parents think, when they offer their children to God in baptism without any due consideration
of the nature of that great covenant with God, that God
must accept, and certainly regenerate and save them!
And I doubt too many religious parents forget that they
themselves are sponsors to that covenant, and that they
undertake to use the means on their part, to make their
children fit for the grace of the Son and the communion of the Spirit; but they think God should sanctify and
preserve them because they are theirs, and are baptized,
though they keep them not from great and unnecessary
temptations, nor plainly and seriously teach them the
meaning of the covenant which was made with God for
them!

How many send their children to get sciences or trades
or to travel in foreign lands before ever they were
instructed at home against those temptations which they
must encounter, and by which they are so often undone!
How commonly, when they have first neglected this
great duty to their children, do they plead a necessity
of thrusting them out from some *punctilio* of honour or
conformity to the world or to adorn them with some of
the plumes of fashionable modes and ceremonies, which
will never compensate the loss of heavenly wisdom,
mortification, and the love of God and man! As if they
might send them to sea for some trifling reason without pilot or anchor, and think that God must save them
from the waves! And when such children have forsaken
God and given themselves up to sensuality and profane-

ness, these parents wonder at the judgments of God and with broken hearts lament their own infelicity instead of lamenting their own misconduct. Thus families, churches, and kingdoms run on to blindness, ungodliness, and confusion. Folly, sin, and misery, misrepresenting themselves as wit, honour, and prosperity, are the ordinary pursuits of mortals. Such a bedlam is most of the world become that he is the bravest man who can sin and be damned with reputation and renown and successfully draw the greatest number with him to hell. This is the world which stands in competition for my love with the spiritual blessed world.

In this world I have had many of God's mercies and comforts; but their sweetness was their taste of divine love, and their tendency to heavenly perfection. What was the end and use of all the good that ever I saw, or that God ever did for my soul or body, but to teach me to love him, and to desire to love him more? Wherever I go and which ever way I look I see vanity and vexation upon all things in this world, so far as they stand in competition with God; and I see holiness to the Lord written upon everything, so far as it leads me to him as my ultimate end. The emptiness, danger, and bitterness of the world, and the all-sufficiency, faithfulness, and goodness of God, have been the sum of all the experiences of my life. And shall a worldly, backward heart overcome the teachings of nature, Scripture, the Spirit of grace, and all experience? O my God, love is thy great and special gift. All good is from thee. Come down into this heart, for it cannot come up to thee! Can the plants go up to the sun for life, or the eye for light? Dwell in me by the Spirit of love and I shall dwell by love in thee. I easily feel that through thy grace I love thy Word, thy image, thy work, and oh, how heartily do I love to love thee, and how I long to know and love thee more!

And if all things are 'of thee, and through thee, and to thee', surely this love is eminently so. It implies thee, Lord. It looks to thee; it serves thee. For thee it moves and seeks and sighs. In thee it trusts. And the hope and peace and comfort which supports me are in thee. When I was a returning prodigal in rags thou sawest me afar off and didst meet me with the caresses of thy love; and shall I doubt whether he that has better clothed me and has dwelt within me will entertain me in the world of love?

The suitableness of things below to my fleshly nature has detained my affections too much on earth; and shall not the suitableness of things above to my spiritual nature much more draw up my love to heaven? *There* is the God whom I have sought and served. He is also *here*; but veiled and little known. *There* he shines to heavenly spirits in heavenly glory. *There* is the Saviour in whom I have believed. He also dwelt on earth; but clothed in such meanness and humbled to such a life and death as was to the Jews a stumbling block, and to the Greeks foolishness. Now he shines and reigns in glory, above the malice and contempt of sinners. And I shall live there, because he lives; and in his light I shall see light. I had here some rays of heavenly light, but under what eclipses, and even long winter nights! *There* I shall dwell in the city of God, the heavenly Jerusalem, where there is no night nor eclipse. *There* are heavenly hosts, in whose holy love and joyful praises I would fain partake. I have here, though unseen, had some of their loving assistance; but there I shall be with them, of the same nature, and the same triumphant church. *There* are perfected souls; not striving, like the disciples, who should be the greatest; not like Noah in the old world; or Lot in Sodom; or Abraham among idol-aters; nor like those that 'wandered about in sheep skins and goat skins, being destitute, afflicted, tormented, hid in dens and caves of the earth'; nor like Job on the dung-hill, or Lazarus at the rich man's gate; nor as we poor bewildered sinners, feeling evil and fearing more.

Should I fear a darksome passage into a world of perfect light? Should I fear to go to Love itself? O excellent grace of faith which foresees, and blessed Word of faith which foreshows, this world of love! Shall I fear to enter where there is no wrath, reserve, suspicion, or self-ish separation; but love will make every holy spirit as dear to me as myself, and me to them as lovely as themselves, and God to us all more amiable than ourselves and all? Lord, hadst thou not given me a will and love, which is part of my nature, I could not have tasted how desir-able it is to live in a world of universal, perfect, endless love. But unless thou also 'sheddest abroad thy love in my heart', by the Spirit of Jesus, the great medium of love, and turn my nature and inclination into divine and holy love, I shall not long for the world of love. O give me not only the image of godliness, but the divine nature, which is holy love! And then my soul will hasten towards thee, and cry, 'How long, O Lord, how long? O come, come quickly, make no delay!'

Surely *the fear of dying* intimates some contrary love that inclines the soul another way, and some shameful unbelief of the attractive glory of the world of love; otherwise no frozen person longs more for the fire, none in a dungeon for light, than we should for heavenly light and love. The love of God to himself is the most amiable object to saints and angels; and next to that, his love to all his works, to the world, and to the church in heaven, manifests more of his loveliness than his love to me. Yet due self-love in me is God's work, and part of his natural image; and when this is grown inordinate by sin I must inquire after God's love to me, for I am not so capable of ascending above self-interest and self-love as I shall be in glory. I am glad to perceive that others love God, and I love those most that I find most love him. But other men's love of God will not be accepted instead of mine. Nor will God's love to others satisfy me without his love to me. But when God's self-love to his creatures, especially the glorified, and also his love to me a vile sinner, are all before me, what should then stay my ascending love, or discourage my desires to be with God?

And canst thou doubt, O my soul, whether thou art going to a God that loveth thee? If the Jews discerned the great love of Christ to Lazarus by his tears, canst not thou discern his love to thee in his blood? It is not the less but the more obliging and amiable that it was not shed for thee alone, but for many. May I not say, I live by the faith of the Son of God, who loved me, and gave himself for me? Yea, it is not so much I that live, but Christ liveth in me. And will he forsake the habitation which his love has chosen, and which he has so dearly bought?

What shall separate us from the love of God? If life has not, death shall not do it. O my soul, if leaning on Christ's breast at meat was a token of his peculiar love to John, is not his dwelling in thee by faith and his living in thee by his Spirit a sure token of his love to thee? Did his dark saying, 'If he tarry till I come, what is that to thee?', raise a report that the beloved disciple should not die? Why should not plain promises assure thee that thou shalt live for ever with him that loveth thee?

Be not so unthankful, O my soul, as to doubt whether thy heavenly Father and thy Lord love thee. Canst thou forget the sealed testimonies of it? Did I not lately repeat so many as ought to shame thy doubt? A multitude of thy friends have so entirely loved thee, that thou canst not doubt of it; and did any of them testify their love with the convicting evidence that God has done? Are *they* love itself? Is *their* love so full, so firm, and unchangeable as his? I think heaven the sweeter because many of my old, lovely, affectionate, holy friends are there, and I am the more willing by death to follow them. And should it not be more pleasing to think that my God and Father, my Saviour and Comforter, are there? Was not Lazarus in the bosom of God? And yet he is said to be in Abraham's bosom; that is, not there alone, but as we are all to sit down with Abraham, Isaac, and Jacob in the kingdom of God. I am often ready to entertain myself with naming such of my friends as are now with Christ; but in heaven they will love me better than they did on earth, and my love to them will be more pleasant. But all these sparks are little to the sun.

Every place I have lived in has its monuments of divine love. Every year and hour of my life has been a time of love. Every friend, neighbour, and even enemy, has been the messenger and instrument of love. Every state and change of my life, notwithstanding my sin, has opened to me the treasures and mysteries of love. And shall I doubt whether the same God loves me? Is he the God of the hills, and not of the valleys? Did he love me in my youth and health, and will he not also in my age and pain and sickness? Did he love all the saints better in their life than at their death?

My groans grieve my friends, but abate not their love. God loved me when I was his enemy, to make me a friend. God will finish his own work. O the multitude of mercies to my soul and body, in peace and war, in youth and age, to myself and friends! Have I lived in the experience of the love of God to me, and shall I die doubting it? I am not much in doubt of the truth of my love to him. I love his Word, works, and ways, and would fain be nearer to him and love him more and loathe myself for loving him no better. Peter may more confidently say, 'Thou knowest that I love thee' than 'I know that thou lovest me';

because our knowledge of God's great love is less than his knowledge of our little love; and without the knowledge of our love to God we can never be sure of his special love to us. I am not entirely a stranger to myself. I know for what I have lived and laboured, and whom I have desired to please. The God 'whose I am, and whom I serve' hath loved me in my youth, and will love me in my aged weakness. My pains seem grievous; but love chooses them, uses them for my good, moderates them, and will shortly end them. Why then should I doubt of my Father's love? Shall pain or dying make me doubt? Did God never love any but Enoch and Elijah? And what am I better than my fathers?

O for a clearer, stronger faith to show me the world that excels this, more than this excels the womb that conceived me! Then I should not fear my third birth-day, for any pangs that precede it. Methinks Daniel's title, 'a man greatly beloved', should be enough to make one joyfully love and trust God, both in life and death. And have not all the saints that title in their degrees? What else signifies their mark, 'holiness to the Lord'? It is but our separation to God as his peculiar, beloved people. And how are we separated but by mutual love? He that is no otherwise beloved than hypocrites and unbelievers, must have his portion with them; and the ungodly, unholy, and unregenerate shall not stand in judgment nor see God nor enter into his kingdom. Upright souls are to blame for their groundless doubts of God's love, not for their acknowledging it, rejoicing in it, or being solicitous to make it sure. Love brought me into the world, furnished me with a thousand mercies, and has provided for me, delivered and preserved me till now; and will it not entertain my separate soul? Is God like false or insufficient friends, that forsake us in adversity?

I confess *I have by sin wronged Love;* but all, except Christ, were sinners whom Love has purified and received to glory. 'God, who is rich in mercy, for his great love wherewith he loved us, even when we were dead in sins, hath quickened us together with Christ, (by grace we are saved,) and hath raised us up together, and made us sit together in heavenly places in Christ Jesus.' O that I could love much, that have been so much forgiven! The glorified praise 'him that loved us, and washed us from our sins in his own blood, and hath made us kings and priests unto God'. Our Father which hath loved us hath given us 'everlasting consolation, and good hope through grace'.

I know no sin which I repent not of with self-loathing, and I earnestly beg and labour that none of my sins may be unknown to me. O that God would bless my accusations, that I may not be unknown to myself, though some think me much better than I am! 'Who can understand his errors?' Lord, 'cleanse thou me from secret faults; keep back thy servant also from presumptuous sins'! I have an Advocate with thee, and I have thy promise, that 'if we confess our sins', thou wilt 'forgive them'. Wherever I have erred, Lord, make it known to me, that my confession may prevent the sin of others; and where I have not erred, confirm and accept me in what is right.

And since an unworthy worm has had so many testimonies of thy love, let me not, when thou sayest, 'I have loved thee', unthankfully ask, 'Wherein hast thou loved me?' Heaven is not more spangled with stars than thy Word and works with the refulgent signatures of love. Thy well-beloved Son, the Son of thy love, who undertook the message and work of thy great love, was full of the spirit of love, which he shed abroad in the hearts of thine elect, that the love of the Father, the grace of the Son, and the communion of the Spirit may be their hope and life. By his workings, sufferings, and gifts, as well as by his comfortable Word, he said to his disciples, 'As the Father loved me, so have I loved you; continue ye in my love.' Lord, how shall we continue in it, but by the thankful belief of thy love and loveliness, desiring still to love thee more, and in all things to know and do thy will, which thou knowest is my soul's desire?

Draw nearer, O my soul, to the Lord of love, and be not seldom and slight in thy contemplation of his love and loveliness. Dwell in the sunshine, and thou wilt know that it is light and warm and comfortable. Distance and strangeness cherish thy doubts. 'Acquaint thyself with him, and be at peace.' Look up, often and earnestly look up, after thy ascended, glorified Head. Think where and what he is, and what he is now doing for all his own, and how once-abased suffering Love is now triumphant, reigning, glorified Love; and therefore is not less now than in all its tender expressions on earth. Had I done this more and better, and as I have persuaded others to do it, I had lived in more convincing delights of God's love, which would have turned the fears of death into more joyful hopes, and more earnest 'desires to be with Christ' as far better, than to be here in a world of darkness, doubts, and fears.

But, O my Father, thou infinite Love, though my arguments be many and strong, my heart is bad, my strength is weakness, and I am insufficient to plead the cause of thy love and loveliness to myself or others. O plead thy own cause, and what heart can resist? Let it not be my word only, but thine, that thou lovest me, even me a sinner! Say as Christ to Lazarus, 'Arise!' Tell me, as thou dost, that the sun is warm, yea, as thou didst, that my parents and dearest friends loved me! Tell me, as by the consciousness and works of life thou tellest me, that thou hast given me life; that while I can say, 'Thou that knowest all things knowest that I love thee', I may infer, 'Therefore I know I am beloved of thee!'

Thus let me come to thee in the confidence of thy love, and long to be nearer, in the clearer sight, the fuller sense, and more joyful exercise of love for ever!
Father, into thy hands I commend my spirit!
Lord Jesus, receive my spirit.
Amen.